INSPIRING OTHERS

DUKE CORPORATE EDUCATION

INSPIRING
OTHERS
WHAT REALLY MOTIVATES PEOPLE

Blair Sheppard • Michael Canning
Marla Tuchinsky • Cindy Campbell

KAPLAN) PUBLISHING

President, Kaplan Publishing: Roy Lipner
Vice President and Publisher: Maureen McMahon
Acquisitions Editor: Michael Cunningham
Development Editor: Trey Thoelcke
Production Editor: Karen Goodfriend
Typesetter: Janet Schroeder
Cover Designer: Design Solutions

Printed in the United States of America

06 07 08   10 9 8 7 6 5 4 3 2 1

Library of Congress Cataloging-in-Publication Data

Duke Corporate Education.
  Inspiring others : what really motivates people / Duke Corporate Education.
      p. cm. — (Leading from the center)
  Includes bibliographical references and index.
  ISBN-13: 978-1-4195-3557-4 (alk. paper)
  ISBN-10: 1-4195-3557-9
  1. Employee motivation.   2. Personnel management.   3. Organizational effectiveness.   I. Title.   II. Series.
  HF5549.5.M63D83 2006
  658.3'14–dc22
                              2006013541

Kaplan Publishing books are available at special quantity discounts to use for sales promotions, employee premiums, or educational purposes. Please call our Special Sales Department to order or for more information at 800-621-9621, ext. 4444, e-mail kaplanpubsales@kaplan.com, or write to Kaplan Publishing, 30 South Wacker Drive, Suite 2500, Chicago, IL 60606-7481.

CONTENTS

ACKNOWLEDGMENTS

First and foremost, we continue to thank our clients and the many program participants around the globe. We begin our work by listening to our clients and gaining an understanding of their business challenges. Working with talented clients and actively engaging in their challenges across a range of industries and geographies has afforded us the opportunity to learn and develop an informed point of view on these topics. We thank our clients for trusting in our approach and making us part of their team. They have shared their experiences and challenges and discussed at length the skills, tools, and mind-sets covered in this book, which has deepened our knowledge and insight.

We also are fortunate to have an extensive network of faculty, coaches, facilitators, and partners who believe in our mission and have opted to join in our adventure. Together, we have delivered programs in 43 different countries since we formed in July of 2000. We absolutely could not have accomplished what we have and learned what we know without their collaboration.

Many thanks also to all of those on the Kaplan Publishing team, who continue to provide valuable feedback and guide us each step of the way. Their assistance and patience through the creation of each book in the *Leading from the Center* series is much appreciated.

We offer special thanks to Dennis Baltzley, who contributed to several of the stories and examples of managers' inspiring others; and to Daniela Silverstein, who shared her experiences in successfully matching nannies and families.

Ryan Stevens again worked to help capture our methods and processes into the graphical images included within the book, often working with vague instructions. As usual, he did a wonderful job.

As always, we could not have accomplished this without the guidance and assistance of our CEO, Blair Sheppard. He supported this initiative from the outset, and more importantly, always made time to review our output and guide our thinking. His assistance is without measure. We could not have done it without him.

We've drawn upon the insight, experience, and expertise from numerous colleagues here at Duke Corporate Education. We hope that the content of this book stimulates your thinking and improves your ability to inspire others.

The *Inspiring Others* team:
Michael Canning, Marla Tuchinsky, Cindy Campbell

INTRODUCTION

In the past 30 years, they have been repeatedly laid off, outsourced, replaced by information technology applications, and insulted with such derogatory names as "the cement layer." Their bosses accused them of distorting and disrupting communication in their organizations, and their subordinates accused them of thwarting the subordinates' autonomy and empowerment. Who are "they"? Middle managers—those managing in the middle of the organization.

With such treatment, you might think that middle managers are villainous evildoers who sabotage companies, or obstructionist bureaucrats who stand in the way of real work getting done. However, the reality is just the opposite. When performed well, the middle manager role is critical in organizations.

Although over the past several decades the value and stature of middle managers has seen both high and low points, we at Duke Corporate Education believe that managing in the center of the organization has always been both critically important and personally demanding. As one would expect, the essence of the role—the required mind-set and skill set—has continued to change over time. The need to update each of these dimensions is driven by periodic shifts in such underlying forces as marketplace dynamics, technology, organizational structure, and employee expectations. Now and then, these forces converge to create a point of inflection that calls for a "step change" in how organizations are governed, with particular implications for those managing in the center.

In the *Leading from the Center* series, we examine some of these primary forces that are shaping what it means to successfully lead from the center in the modern organization. We outline the emerging imperative for middle management in an organization as well as the mind-set, knowledge, and skills required to successfully navigate the most prevalent challenges that lie ahead.

THE NEW CENTER

Four powerful and pervasive trends affect the role that managers in the center of an organization are asked to assume. These trends—information technology, industry convergence, globalization, and regulations—connect directly to the challenges these managers face.

Compared to 20 or 30 years ago, *information technology* has escalated the amount, speed, and availability of data and has changed the way we work and live. Access to information has shifted more power to our customers and suppliers. They not only have more information but are directly involved in and interacting with the various processes along the value chain. On a personal level, we now find ourselves connected to other people all the time; cell phones, pagers, BlackBerrys, and PDAs all reinforce the 24/7 culture. The transition from workweek to weekend and back is less distinct. Instead, microtransitions happen all day, every day, because many of us remain connected all the time.

Industries previously seen as separate are now seeing multiple points of *convergence*. Think about how digital technology has led to a convergence of sound, image, text, computing, and communications. Long-standing industry boundaries and parameters are gone (e.g., cable television companies are in the phone business, and electronics companies sell music) and along with them, the basis and nature of competition. When boundaries are blurred, new possibilities, opportunities, and directions exist, but it isn't always clear what managers should do. Managers will have to be prepared to adapt; their role is to observe, learn from experience, and set direction dynamically. Layered on top of this is the need to manage a more complex set of relationships—cooperating on Monday, competing on Tuesday, and partnering on Wednesday.

Globalization means that assets are distributed and configured around the world to serve customers and gain competitive advantage. Even companies that consider themselves local interact with global organizations. There is more reliance on fast-developing regional centers of expertise (e.g., computer programming in India and manufacturing in China). This means that middle managers are interacting with and coordinating the efforts of people who live in different cultures and may even be awake while their managers are asleep. The notion of a workday has changed as the work spans time zones. The nature of leading has changed as partnering with vendors and working in virtual teams across regions become more common.

The first three forces are causing shifts in the fourth—the *regulatory environment*. Many industries are experiencing more regulation, while a few others are experiencing less. Some arenas experiencing more regulation are also encountering a drive for more accountability. Demand for more accountability leads to a greater desire to clarify boundaries and roles, yet both the rules and how best to operationalize them are more ambiguous than ever. Consider how, in the wake of Sarbanes-Oxley legislation, U.S. companies and their accountants continue to sort through the new requirements, while rail companies in Britain are negotiating which company is responsible for maintaining what stretch of tracks. Middle managers sit where regulations get implemented and are a critical force in shaping how companies respond to the shifts in the environment.

All of these changes have implications for those managing at the center of organizations. No small group at the top can have the entire picture, because the environment has more of everything: more information and connectivity, a faster pace, a dynamic competitive space, greater geographic reach, better informed and connected customers and suppliers, and shifting legal rules of the game. No small group can process the implications, make thoughtful decisions, and disseminate clear action steps. The top of the organization needs those in the center to help make sense of the dynamic environment. The connection between strategy development and strategy execution becomes less linear and more interdependent, and, therefore, managers in the center become pivotal actors.

As we said earlier, the notion of the middle of an organization typically conjures up a vertical image depicting managers in the center of a hierarchy. This mental image carries with it a perception of those managers as gatekeepers—controlling the pace at which information or resources flow down or up. It appears simple and linear.

However, as many of you are no doubt experiencing, you find yourselves navigating in a matrix and as a node in a network or multiple networks. As depicted in Figure 1.1, this new view of the center conjures up images of centrality, integration, connection, and catalyst. *You are in the center of the action, not the middle of a hierarchy.*

FIGURE I.I Center of the Action

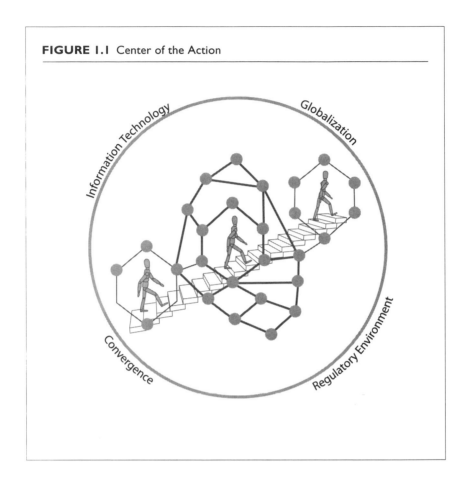

When you overlay this connected view on the traditional vertical notion, it produces some interesting tensions, trade-offs, and opportunities. Your formal authority runs vertically, but your real power to achieve results stems from your ability to work across all levels and boundaries.

IF YOU ARE LEADING FROM THE CENTER

If you are a manager in the center today, you have many hats to wear, more balls to juggle, and fewer certainties in your work environment. You have to be adaptive yet provide continuity in your leadership. You need to simultaneously translate strategy, influence and collaborate, lead teams, coach and motivate, support innovation, and own the systems and processes—all in the service of getting results. Those in the center need more courage than ever. You are the conscience of your organization, carrying forth its values, and at the same time you build today's and tomorrow's business success.

Strategy Translator

As a strategy translator, you must first understand the corporate strategy and determine what parts of it your group can best support. Next, you must translate it into an action plan for your group, making sure it aligns well to the overall strategy. You'll need to consider which projects are essential stepping stones and which are needed in their own right, and establish some priorities or guiding goals. You must then communicate the details of the plan and priorities and create momentum around them. As your team implements, you'll need not only to involve your people but also to collaborate and coordinate with others, including peers, customers, and other units. Instead of directing a one-way downward flow of information, you must translate upward as well and act as a conduit for strategic feedback to the executives above.

Influencer and Collaborator for Results

Middle managers must learn how to make things happen by influencing, integrating, and collaborating across the boundaries of the organization. As a manager, instead of focusing exclusively on your piece, you have to look outside of your own group to develop a network of supporting relationships. Rather than issuing commands and asserting power based on your position, you have to use other tactics to gain agreement and make things happen.

Leader of Teams

Teams have become a one-size-fits-all solution for organizing work in today's economy—virtual teams, project teams, product teams, and function-specific teams—and can be either the blessing or the bane of many companies. Your role as a manager includes understanding the challenges of teams and facilitating their development so that they can be effective more quickly. You have to align the team's energy and talents in a way that will deliver the desired results. You are responsible for creating an environment that will help this group of people work well together to achieve today's objectives and to develop the skills needed to take on future goals.

Coach and Motivator

Many organizations are well positioned to execute their strategies in yesterday's environment, are moderately able to meet their current needs, and often are not thinking at all about how to position themselves for the future. From the center of the organization, middle managers assume much of the responsibility for their people. They create an environment to attract and retain good employees, coach them to do their current jobs better, and bear primary responsibility for developing others. As a manager, you must figure out how to build the next level of capability, protect existing people, connect their aspirations to opportunities for development, and make work more enjoyable. You need to provide regular feedback—both positive and redirecting—and build strong relationships with those who surround you. If you do your job well, your departments will be more efficient, and your employees will be better equipped to become leaders in their own right.

Intrapreneur/Innovator

Enabling and supporting an innovative approach within your company will foster the strategic direction of the future. To effectively sponsor innovation, you need to create the context for your people, foster a climate that supports innovative efforts, and actively sponsor the ideas of the future. You have to be innovative and lead the innovative efforts of others. Innovation is most often associated with new-product development, but innovative approaches also are needed in developing new services or solving internal system and process problems. As a manager, you use your influence and relationships to find the root cause of problems and the resources to make change happen.

Owner of Systems and Processes

You need to understand that part of your role is to take ownership for designing and building new systems and processes. You will have to shift your thinking from living within existing systems and processes to making sure that those systems and processes work well: Do the systems and processes support progress or get in its way? One of the mistakes we have made in the past is not to hold managers accountable for their role in building the next generation of systems and processes. As a manager, you must perform harsh audits of existing systems and understand when to tear down what may have been left in place from a past strategy. You need to assess what is no longer relevant and/or is no longer working. Part of your responsibility is to evaluate and decide whether to reengineer or remove existing systems.

SHIFTS IN MIND-SET NEEDED FOR THE FUTURE

As a manager you assume a responsibility for developing and retaining the organization's talent, coaching others to do their jobs better, and getting results through others. You need motivated people who bring a level of energy, commitment, and creativity to their jobs. Simply telling them what to do isn't enough, but you are at a loss as to how to discover and tap into what motivates them and inspires them to do their best work.

It's not for lack of suggested approaches that you struggle. Researchers and theorists have defined many *potential* motivators—equity, job security, advancement, self-esteem, degree of challenge, sense of belonging, peer recognition, financial reward—and how to best use them in practice. Their original tenets make sense but people and times are changing and motivators aren't always easily applied in today's dynamic workplace.

What *can* you do to develop inspired people? As you have probably already discovered, there is no single answer that works for all. Inspiring others requires a new mind-set and a new approach. This book will guide you through a new formula that suggests beginning with understanding the individual and then adapting situations to meet his or her needs, rather than beginning with what you need or the organization needs and trying to adapt people to fit the situation.

CHAPTER ONE

THE CHALLENGE OF INSPIRING OTHERS

IN THIS CHAPTER

Why Do People . . . ? ■ The Business Case: Why Bother? ■
Looking Forward

WHY DO PEOPLE . . . ?

Why is it that people don't do what I ask them to do? Why do they seem so disconnected from their work? Why don't they show any initiative?

When it comes to understanding the behaviors and actions of their people, managers may find themselves frequently asking why. Considering that the manager is "the boss," shouldn't people jump up and eagerly follow the manager's directions? If not, why not? The simple answer is that people are motivated in different ways. They aren't motivated because you want them to be, or because you praise them, or because you threaten them, or because you set challenging goals for them.

Why *do* people do what they do? According to psychologist John Atkinson,

$$\text{Behavior} = f(\text{person} + \text{situation}).$$

In other words, people behave based on who they are and the circumstances they find themselves in. Behavior is a function of an individual acting in a particular situation. The same person will behave differently in a variety of situations; different people will have different reactions to the same situation; and the way they behave today isn't necessarily how they'll behave in the future because both people and situations are constantly changing (Kelner 2000).

What does this imply for managers? People are complex; what motivates one means little to another; what provides inspiration for one person may fall flat with another. You can't treat everyone exactly the same and expect uniform results. Job assignments are tricky because people have different preferences, and may not be motivated to do what they're asked. Yet, you still need to achieve certain results. What's it going to take for you to inspire the behavior that leads to good results?

Look at the behavior equation again. Logic tells you that you can influence either the person or the situation to have an effect on behavior. Ethics aside for the moment, in most cases it will be easier to shape the situation than to shape the person. Manipulating people isn't a viable long-term strategy (and is dicey short term, too). Instead, you *can* match people to situations where they can perform well. It's hard to change people to fit the environment, so that leaves changing the situation.

That doesn't mean that you can ignore the person, concentrate all of your energy on changing the environment, and expect success. *For our purposes, motivation comes from inside a person; inspiration comes from outside a person.* Much inspiration comes from the world we observe and live in. Photographers may find inspiration in unique lighting and angles, artists may find inspiration in scenic landscapes, and authors may find inspiration in the everyday events or stories of life. Many find inspiration in learning more about those who share their passion for something, or have overcome their own obstacles, and often have wisdom to share.

For example, Olympic athletes are motivated to compete; in their hearts and minds, they want to win, to be the best. This is how, as any coach will tell you, they are all very different individuals. Their coach's role is to teach skills, but also to understand each athlete and what helps to inspire that individual to keep going—showing

how he or she can win; reminding the athlete why he or she is working so hard; and changing the situation by implementing new practice routines or locations, setting new goals, changing their
approaches, and offering support. The coaches help to inspire, but
it's an intrinsic love of the game, desire to compete, or personal drive
that gets those athletes to cooperate, practice, and give it their all.
Coaches often can identify those athletes who have no lack of talent
or potential, but who don't have the internal motivation it takes to
move to the next level.

Like a coach, your role as a manager is to understand, support,
guide, and inspire the people you lead, and to build on the motivation
that exists within each person. It's only by first knowing the person that
you can then understand *how* to shape the situation, so he or she has
the right context in which to excel at work. If you know your people
well, you can tap into their energy, skills, and enthusiasm by creating an
environment that fits them. You create a setting that supports the particular elements that inspire team members to their best performance
and what it is that they love to do. Thus, the equation becomes:

Understand the person + Adapt the environment =
Inspired behavior

THE BUSINESS CASE: WHY BOTHER?

Having inspired and motivated employees is critical to staying in
business; it is a key to both engaging and enabling them to do their
best work and then retaining that talent. Motivated individuals (including you, the manager) feed their own enthusiasm into inspired
and collaborative teams that form the units of a successful organization. It can be a virtuous cycle, resulting in high-quality outputs, innovation, and great performance. However, it also can be a
downward spiral, when people who are bored, frustrated, or disen-
gaged achieve only minimum performance and potentially bring the
rest of their team down as well. Your ability to inspire and engage the
individuals you lead is critical to the company's success.

This is true all across an organization—in line roles, back-office
jobs, or customer-facing positions. James Oakley, a Purdue Univer-

sity assistant professor of marketing, has shown a direct link between employee satisfaction and customer satisfaction, and between customer satisfaction and financial performance—even when those employees have no direct contact with customers (Oakley 2004). If you can inspire your people, they tend to have higher job satisfaction, which translates to positive business performance.

Engaged, challenged, and inspired employees are also less likely to leave. At the team level, retention saves the cost and disruption of replacing well-trained, well-integrated people with new but inexperienced talent. The team can avoid the typical loss of momentum that occurs when people adjust their routines and tasks to accommodate a new member.

Today, very few companies feel they have an excess of talent. Retention of the best talent provides a much broader pool from which they can internally develop the organization's future leaders, rather than being forced to go outside over and over. It's estimated that companies spent as much as $50 billion on talent development in 2005. Across many industries today, companies are in a real battle to attract, develop, and retain the best talent, a resource that is becoming scarce in some areas. For cxamplc, oil field services giant Schlumberger is finding engineering talent at a premium. Often recognized as a company that dedicates extensive resources to talent development, they also put equal effort into exploring any loss of talent. The departure of a high-performance person is seen as the same level as a catastrophic accident, and they investigate the causes as deeply as they would a technical mistake that caused hours of expensive downtime on an oil rig. The results of exit interviews are shared online, available to managers throughout the organization (*BusinessWeek Online,* October 10, 2005).

LOOKING FORWARD

In this book, we'll explore what really works and how you can effectively apply the principles of this new behavior equation in the workplace. In Chapter 2, we'll look at how some popular motivation theories have played out in practice and how their flaws have become more pronounced under the pressures of the modern world; and we'll offer some guiding principles for a new era.

CHAPTER TWO

NEW APPROACH FOR A NEW ERA

IN THIS CHAPTER

What We've Been Led to Believe ■ The Myths in Practice ■
New Guiding Principles

WHAT WE'VE BEEN LED TO BELIEVE

The theories about what really drives people's behavior, and thus what managers can do to develop and sustain their motivation, span a wide spectrum. Needs theories have focused on *what* motivates people to choose certain behaviors, process theories have focused more on *how* the process takes place, and reinforcement theories have explored what can be done to increase the likelihood that behavior will change or stay the same. Some followed an assumption that work by its very nature is unpleasant and not motivating; therefore, people work for other reasons. This implied that making money was more important than the particular task. In other words, if people were unmotivated, then organizations could pay them more and solve the motivation problem with a checkbook.

Other theories told us that people's sense of belonging and feeling useful were more powerful motivators than money, and so managers worked to make their people feel that they were part of a larger team, and that their role was as important as every other role in working to meet the organization's goals. Motivational campaigns depicted all who had a hand in assembling the automobile, delivering the package, or helping the plane depart and arrive on time as critical parts of the process. The implications were that everyone was equally important and thus equally motivated to achieve the same goal; pay rates played a lesser role because pride would make up for salary shortfalls.

Still others proposed that people inherently *wanted* to use their talents to make real contributions, and what most motivated them was a challenging job that gave them a feeling of achievement, responsibility, growth, and enjoyment of work itself. Therefore, it was the organization's responsibility to create an environment that made the best use of their resources and talent while at the same time still focused on the organization's needs and goals.

These researchers and theorists explored many of the same *potential* motivators, such as equity, fairness, safety, security, advancement, esteem, challenge, belonging, recognition, reward, and, of course, the paycheck. Their theories weren't necessarily wrong about what *can be* motivating to people, but *our experience suggests that, while well intentioned and useful, they share some inherent flaws about how motivation works and the manager's role in the process.*

- *They begin with a central misconception that if some individuals lack motivation then it's possible for you, the manager, to find ways to create it for them.* When managers describe an employee as unmotivated, what they really mean is that the individual isn't motivated to behave in the way the managers would like. As long as a person makes choices and puts forth some amount of effort, he or she is, by definition, motivated. A teenager who spends his evening playing video games in pursuit of the high score, rather than doing schoolwork, is surely motivated. It's just not by the activities or goals his parents want him focused on, such as good grades, broader perspective, admission to college, and a degree that leads to a well-paying job. The other half of this misconception is that one person can directly change what motivates another. The parent who has tried any number of tactics (rewards, punishments, study aids) to no avail can attest to that. There may be a temporary shift in behavior, but it's not likely to stick if the person just doesn't want to do it.

- *They share a proposition that the job of the manager is to foist onto people what the manager or organization wants done.* True, it is part of a manager's job to get work done through others; however, this approach says managers need to understand why people do things (i.e., what motivates them) only enough so they can persuade those people to work toward the goals of the organization. The idea was basically to align what *you* need people to do with what you can convince people to do, by using whatever technique is most effective—buying, conning, or forcing them—to get results. This pragmatic approach may also work for the short term, but it isn't sustainable. It's expensive, and you may run into trouble later. This approach perpetuates the image of the boss as a person who does things *to* employees rather than someone who works *with* employees. Another danger of this approach is that if managers drive people where they don't want to be, the employees may form unions or isolate themselves in resistance. This approach makes performance reviews hard, too, because it starts from the manager saying you didn't meet *my* (the manager's) needs.

- *They view motivation more in terms of single transactions rather than in terms of sustainable, long-term relationships.* Focusing on the transaction—the single goal that you are trying to achieve—tends to lead managers and others into forgetting the other things they want and need to accomplish or the other interests and aspirations that people have beyond the current task. When the immediate work is completed or the current crisis resolved, it may end with a "pat on the back" and little or no exploration as to what the person found engaging or uninteresting in the work, what she managed easily or thought difficult, or what she discovered she would like to do more of. The relationship between manager and team member often suffers as a result. Once the relationship begins to erode (or never reaches a reasonable level of trust), managers have to turn their attention to rebuilding the relationship and focusing on "loyalty" as an explicit aim.

- *They were interesting ideas with intuitive appeal, but validating them and applying them was challenging.* There is wisdom in these theories of motivation, but they have been difficult to prove empirically. For example, Freud argued that we are not even consciously aware of many of the factors affecting our behavior. Maslow's five-level hierarchy of needs theory (1943), that people first meet basic needs (food, water, oxygen) and then are motivated to satisfy progressively higher needs (safety, love, belonging, recognition, mastery) sounds reasonable, but has yet to be validated. Applying motivation theories has been further complicated by the fact that each person brings unique life experiences into any situation, and we operate in a dynamic work environment that continues to change. Those unique experiences and situations shape how people behave, and that isn't predictable from most of the theories.

© Mike Baldwin / Cornered

"Worked all weekend to finish the report, and all I get is a stupid Pat on the back."

www.CartoonStock.com

THE MYTHS IN PRACTICE

Motivated employees bring a level of energy, commitment, and creativity to their jobs. So it's no surprise that as the business environment has become more competitive, searching for the answer to what it takes to build a motivated workforce has become a focal point for organizations and the managers who direct them.

Without a doubt, how to foster inspired and motivated people is a good problem on which to spend energy. Managers have been offered several reasonable theories for solving the problem, but in practice find that flaws in the approaches get even more pronounced over time. They may be effective in changing someone's behavior during a single instance but have no real lasting effect on the internal motivators that drive the individual. Yet we continue trying under the belief that we can find that magic formula that will work for everyone and get people to do what *we* want them to do.

Myth 1: The Silver Bullet: Fix the Reward

Show me the money! has become a well-known line from the movie *Jerry McGuire,* a film that tells the story of a football player who wants and demands the same multimillion-dollar contract the other star players are receiving. As the movie progresses, we realize the character isn't motivated by money itself but by his desire to achieve future financial security for his family while still able to play the game. A lucrative and signed contract is a means to provide what he really needs. Many people have adopted this catchphrase in jest, implying to bosses or coworkers, "If you pay me the big bucks, I'll deliver." Money may be a placeholder for something different in their lives, but these workers echo the myth that people's effort can be bought.

One early motivation process theory was the expectancy theory, developed by Victor Vroom. He contended that motivation is based on how much we want something and how likely we think we are to get it. The theory proposes three variables:

1. **Expectancy:** If I try, can I do it?
2. **Instrumentality:** If I do it, will I get the expected outcome?
3. **Valence:** Do I really value the available outcomes?

For example, your only means of transportation is an old clunker that is quickly reaching the end of its days. The reward for submitting the best process improvement idea is a new car. If you believe your idea has a good chance of winning, you are more motivated to act—you think you can do it, you trust the contest organizers will in fact award the car, and you yourself value that car. Porter and Lawler's Expectancy Model later extended Vroom's theory, contending that the actual process was much more complex than originally depicted. For example, they noted that increased effort doesn't automatically lead to improved performance if someone doesn't have the required skills or doesn't understand how to do the tasks. In this case, an individual could put forth a lot of effort without the results to show for it (Porter and Lawler 1968).

Using extrinsic rewards and recognition as a motivating source is based on a belief that individuals can be motivated if their behavior will lead to an outcome that they desire, such as salary, security, or personal recognition. An exchange takes place if the employee asks, *"What do they want me to do, what do I get in return, and is it something I care about?"*, and likes the answer. Within the workplace, this approach plays out in companywide plans for merit pay, commissions, profit sharing, bonuses, and promotions. For example, companies assume that the promise of sharing a company's profits is enough of an incentive to drive employees' performance to a target level; if the company benefits, employees benefit as well.

There are several inherent problems in this approach. People are driven by their own intrinsic motivators; therefore, the effects of rewards and recognition are limited in scope, short-lived, and have little or no lasting effect on their motivation. When little or no motivation exists, people are likely to go only as far as required to achieve the reward (if they actually want it), and typically revert back to their old behavior once the reward or recognition stops. Once you reach the minimum sales target, there is not as much incentive to keep going. Once you have the new car, any reason to behave in a certain way is gone.

One of the early motivation theorists, Frederick Herzberg, used the analogy of a dog: If you want the dog to move, you can give him a nudge from behind or you can lead him to a new spot by offering a treat. Either way, it creates more work for you, because every time

"DEXTER GOT A GOLDEN PARACHUTE, NOLAN GOT A GOLDEN HANDSHAKE AND I GOT A GOLDEN RETRIEVER."

Reprinted with permission of Sidney Harris

you want the dog to move, *you* have to expend time and energy doing something. The end result is the dog is no more motivated to move to the desired spot on later attempts than he was the first. He may move if you keep nudging or buying treats, but wouldn't it be better for everyone if the dog selected the spot where *he* most wanted to be and moved by himself? (Herzberg 1993).

On the other hand, when driven by intrinsic motivation, the rewards and accolades are secondary. Consider how many actors spend their lives going to auditions, doing summer stock theatre, and taking small roles in TV or movies, just to continue working as actors. They aren't rich; few people outside their families and friends would know their names. Yet, they keep at it, following their dreams and their passion. There are research scientists who persevere for years, because they want to answer a question, not because they may win a Nobel Prize. There are writers who will never win a Pulitzer, a Booker, or a National Book Award, and yet they keep producing. In each case, the inner interest and fire keep them working and trying. Do they appreciate recognition for their efforts or contributions when it comes? Certainly, but it's not necessarily what drove them to get there.

Myth 2: Fear Really Does Work

Using fear to convince people to change has been a widely used tactic across time, industries, and interests. Health campaigns seek to convince people to alter their lifestyle, eating habits, or stress levels because it will (eventually) damage their bodies. Environmental interests admonish us to stop polluting so that we have a clean environment to pass on to future generations, or to conserve resources before they are depleted. Police and legal codes warn us about the punishments we can receive for any number of infractions.

Fear of potential consequences does actually cause us to change our behavior, but be clear that *compliance* is not the same as *commitment*. The promise of what *could* happen if we don't perform as expected may be strong enough to persuade us to comply with rules or do the minimum we've been asked. The problem is that people tend to do just enough to avoid punishment, but are not inclined to give any extra amount of discretionary effort, as we would for those things we do willingly. Because employers can buy or scare people into the letter of compliance, discretionary effort extending to the spirit of a request becomes even more valuable.

Like rewards and recognition, fear of consequences can achieve short-term results in the workplace, but also can produce lasting damage to the employee/manager relationship. The threat of the repercussions for failing may build resentment in employees and create an adversarial relationship. Your employees can become not only unenthusiastic and uninspired, but may lose feelings of goodwill and loyalty toward you or your business.

Myth 3: Cascade the Objectives, and Everyone Will Fall in Line

The popular management by objectives approach begins with the needs of the organization and then focuses on improving performance and results by aligning their resources to achieve those goals and objectives. Each layer hands down a set of goals or targets to those who are one layer lower in the hierarchy. Rather than relying on good intentions, the process asks the manager and employee to agree on what the employee will try to achieve within a particular time period, and to write those objectives down for future reference and evaluation. The manager monitors the employee's progress, then evaluates the person's performance relative to his peers or other performance standards, rewards his high achievements, and sets new objectives with the employee to begin the cycle anew.

In this approach, the focus is more on assigning tasks and getting results than on whether people are motivated by their work. People may meet some of their own needs and preferences because they are allowed some flexibility in *how* they approach their tasks, but not in which ones they elect to do. Managers clearly define the objectives, but where in this process do managers learn more about what motivates their people, and which tasks will get them truly engaged and excited by their work? Setting goals and having a person agree to them may be sufficient to drive people to achieve the minimum; however, it may not get the person to go beyond that, even if capable of it.

Certainly, we agree that alignment and clear objectives are important, but they can take people only so far. Individuals and teams need to know how they connect to the larger strategy and be inspired by what it is they are trying to accomplish because demands, priorities, and objectives are usually in flux. Problems can occur when managers aren't thoughtful about work assignments, don't create roles that match people well, and think they're done once they've delivered the objectives to their people. Managers may think, "Now it's up to my team." In reality, their work is just starting. Consider the greater possibilities, both for the company and individuals, if people were matched and aligned with work that was highly engaging and motivating to them, and thus were proactive in responding to new challenges as they occur.

NEW GUIDING PRINCIPLES

If your actions inspire others to dream more, learn more, do more, and become more, you are a leader.
John Quincy Adams

If there is no magic formula for motivating others that will solve all your problems, what can and should you do? You can't take the organization and work that needs to get done completely out of the picture, but starting there is starting in the wrong place. Inspiring people is complex because each person and situation has unique aspects. Start with the individual and keep the following four guiding principles in mind as you work with your employees.

1. Know your people, and build around their aspirations, strengths, and needs. At the heart of our advice to managers is to begin your efforts to inspire employees with a deeper knowledge of who they are—their ambitions, personalities, preferences, talents, and interests. Inspiration comes not from manipulating employee preferences through systems of compensation, intimidation, or benefits, but through understanding them and situating their work appropriately. Think of this as a process of discovery. Learn more about the things that they are currently good at, and invest in those talents. Understand what they aspire to do in the future and match them with opportunities to develop skills that will help them reach those goals. Give them options that let them express their preferences and interests.

At some level, people need some sense of *achievement, affiliation,* and *power*. A manager has to address these core needs for people, and recognize that they will vary based on each individual's unique life experiences and personality. People want to feel that their work is challenging, that they have accomplished something valuable, and that their efforts result in something useful or important. They need to feel a part of a group or organization. We are social beings and often look to our work environment as a place to interact with others. For some, being able to influence and guide others or to have an effect on the organization are strong needs (McClelland 1988). Finally, they also wish to feel that others treat them with dignity and respect. A manager's task is to create a workplace where individuals can meet their particular needs as part of their work experience.

2. Expect excellence and treat people like owners. In a classic 1968 experiment, researchers randomly chose 20 percent of the children from a classroom and told the teachers they were "intellectual bloomers" who were expected to show great progress during the year. The result? The "intellectual bloomers" really did bloom (Rosenthal and Jacobson 1968). This self-fulfilling prophecy plays out not only in classroom interactions between teachers and students, but between managers and employees. We tend to form expectations of people and, consciously or not, tip people off to what our expectations are. People in turn adjust their behavior to match, and the original expectation becomes true.

Rather than create an environment that implies employees are not to be trusted and should be closely monitored and controlled so they do no harm, instead create an environment that conveys that you expect them to make good decisions, to excel at what they do, and to achieve great results. Expect them to behave like "owners." As owners, provide them information about how the company is doing and their relationship to that performance. Teach shareholder value to illustrate those linkages. Finally, live with the questions and challenges that come with excellence and ownership.

3. Understand where people are in their journey. Each stage, or chapter, in life shifts people's priorities and focus. Someone just out of college and living alone for the first time has a different focus than someone who is 15 years into a career. Someone in midlife may suddenly find himself caring for an ailing parent while someone soon to retire might feel a greater desire to develop other skills (Erikson 1993). As a manager, recognize the chapter people are in and how this plays out in their choices—lifestyle, family commitments, work interests, and aspirations—and what motivates them. If you misjudge where they are or don't recognize when they are in a transition period, it drastically alters your ability to inspire and their ability to respond.

Each person has experienced a different series of events and themes in arriving where they are today. If you don't know some fundamental, important events that have shaped or are still shaping their lives, you can't know what motivates them. These experiences are elemental to the person they are. To be an effective manager, you must care enough to build a relationship with each of your people. You need to get to know them as individuals, and form a basis of trust within which they are willing to share some of the details of their personal stories. These stories offer insight into what motivates them or puts them off. Once you understand, you can help connect their core interests, needs, and values to the work that they do.

4. Don't wait—get started. This may be new ground for you and your people. You may be apprehensive about how to start the conversation or how people will react and respond. Focus on getting the basics right and the rest will follow. Realize that it's likely that you are better at it than you think, but it still may be hard. You'll have to get past the "excuses" that managers typically have:

- "Asking about someone's private life is illegal and irrelevant."
- "I'm not a psychologist."
- "What if their needs don't align to the work we need to get done?"
- "This company is too big to create this kind of culture."

If you understand and agree with the guiding principles, how do you apply them on a daily basis? You might say, "I manage a variety of people and deal with all types of situations and problems, and I'm still expected to get results for the company. Meeting people's needs is nice, but I have targets to hit." If, as a manager, you can't create or maintain what motivates another, what's the answer? What you *can* do is understand their internal motivators, connect them with the situations and opportunities that are most interesting and energizing to them, and then create an environment that allows them the flexibility to achieve results in ways that best meet their needs.

In the next four chapters, we offer some specific advice on how to put these guiding principles into practice. In Chapter 3, we discuss knowing the whole person—what it means and how to connect people to opportunity. Motivation comes from within; as a manager, you can tap into it by working with people's energy. In Chapter 4, we explain precisely why some large industries are failing—they've created a work environment antithetical to positive performance—and how you can create an inspiring environment for your people. In Chapter 5, we use the performance review conversation as an example of a very commonly missed opportunity. Instead of an adversarial, judgmental conversation, this should be a chance to inspire people. Finally, in Chapter 6, we bring it all together and talk about how to sustain the enthusiasm.

CHAPTER THREE

KNOWING THE
WHOLE PERSON

IN THIS CHAPTER

Start with the Person ■ Be a Matchmaker ■
Yesterday, Today, Tomorrow ■ Build the Relationship ■
Getting Work Done

Understand the Person + Adapt the Environment
= Inspired Behavior

If inspired behavior is the end result that we want to achieve, we should begin with understanding the individual. Recall one of the most engaging and enjoyable times that you've experienced at work. For one person, it may be probing a piece of broken machinery or searching for the error in a string of software code until the problem is discovered and remedied. For another, it may be explaining a complex topic to a group of students and seeing their flash of insight. For someone else, it may be resolving a difficult customer issue, delivering a persuasive presentation, or coaching a team member as she works to master a new skill. In those moments, everything just clicks. Psychologist Mihaly Csikszentmihalyi describes these as "flow experiences," when we become oblivious to external distractions and get completely engrossed in the task, often losing track of time. The work may be so challenging and consuming that you skip lunch or stay late because you don't want to interrupt the flow. The old saying, "Time flies when you're having fun," captures the feeling. It may be hard to describe, but you know it when you experience it (Csikszent-mihalyi, 1997).

The activities that are intrinsically motivating are those that we would do without any external persuasion, what we find most inter-esting and enjoyable. To be sure, not all tasks lead to flow experi-ences, but we still feel positive about completing the work. As we learned in Chapter 2, this is what motivates people—doing activities they find interesting, satisfying, rewarding, or enjoyable. It takes lit-tle to inspire them to do those actions, because they really want to do them. There is no conflict between what they want and what you want from them.

One of our authors often asks people interviewing for a job the following question: "There are parts of my job that I absolutely love and would do for free, and other parts that they pay me to do. Which parts of your job would you do for free?" The idea is that the tasks they would do for free are the ones they find most motivating and where they think their talents are best used. They are excited to do those particular tasks.

It seems, then, that to the extent we can get people doing what they feel best suited for and most excited to take on, we will largely solve the problem of inspiring them, because their natural energy and passion for the work takes over. *Consider what they find most en-gaging and want to do and then match that with what the organization needs to achieve.* Work with the inherent drive and motivation that people have, aligning it to fulfill the outcomes you need. This seems synergistic, so why doesn't it happen more?

START WITH THE PERSON

One reason that this natural alignment isn't used to our advan-tage more often is that most managers—at all levels—take the organi-zation as their starting point. First, they set out what results their team or division needs to deliver for the company and spend consid-erable time defining what capabilities they'll need to accomplish their goals—resources, skills, talents, and the like. Next, managers focus on figuring out how to mold their people to match those needs. If someone doesn't match, they either send her for training to make her match better or hire someone else. This common approach, though, tries to shape the *people* to better fit the *organization*.

However, consider what would happen if you flipped that approach on its head: Start with the people, and try to shape the organization to meet their needs instead. Of course, the work still need needs to get done; but people who are better matched to their work will deliver better results. Get to know your team: What are their talents, interests, aspirations, and experience? What type of activities do they find most motivating? Knowing that, think about how you can assign tasks to best take advantage of what they love to do and are good at. Some of those may be tasks within your team; others may be opportunities to contribute to larger-scale projects in other areas of the organization. As Figure 3.1 indicates, some tasks may not connect at all to their interests or talents, some may be a partial

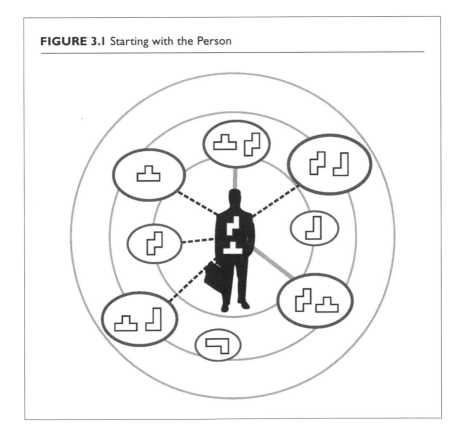

FIGURE 3.1 Starting with the Person

fit and offer a chance to experience new areas, and some may seem to be just the opportunity that will fully engage them.

For example, a drugstore manager talked about the different tasks that needed to be done in her store, such as stocking shelves, helping customers, checking prices, and running registers. Traditionally, people were assigned a particular task for a shift and rotated to another in the next shift. The idea was that no one had to do the less desirable tasks all the time; everyone took a turn doing everything. What the manager realized, though, was that she had people with different preferences that were unlikely to change and skills that weren't being used to their full advantage. Joe, for example, was happiest stocking shelves. He found it satisfying to create order, and loved checking price tags for the same reason. Customers, though, irritated him and he tried to avoid them whenever possible. Frieda, on the other hand, was terrific with customers and knew many of them by name. She was wonderful helping people with their selections and was always a friendly face at the register. The monotony of checking shelf tags, however, made her crazy, and she tended to make mistakes. The manager quickly realized that randomly rotating her staff across *all* the jobs meant that *someone* was always matched with doing something he or she didn't like (and perhaps not doing it very well). Instead, the manager created smaller rotation pools and organized people by their talents and preferences; for example, she gave Joe twice as many stocking rotations and little register time and gave Frieda twice as many customer-service rotations as shelf tag-checking shifts. In this way, the manager still provided some variety for her people but also matched them more often to the work they preferred and enjoyed. The result? The work got done, customers were satisfied, and people made fewer mistakes and were rarely absent from work.

If you start with people and where they are, you then can better match them to opportunities and influence the environment around them. Shifting the situation will be a much easier way to influence the behaviors you want than trying to change the person (more on that in the next chapter). So, *what does it mean to start with people?*

- Beginning at the hiring phase, try to find people whose interests and aspirations are a good fit with the needs of your team and organization

- Build relationships with your employees to understand their experience and life stage
- Have conversations to understand your employees' strengths and aspirations
- Match those aspirations and talents to opportunities

What motivates people will vary wildly, but it comes from within. To be able to connect to a person's fundamental needs and create work that matches his or her own motivation, you have to know the whole person.

BE A MATCHMAKER

Matchmaker, Matchmaker
Look through your book,
And make me a perfect match.
Sheldon Harnick, *Fiddler on the Roof*

Whether choosing people to join an existing group, formatting a new team, or organizing your existing staff to take on a new piece of work, managers should try to be good matchmakers. Begin by understanding the team's and the organization's needs, and then seek people whose needs and skills will be a good fit. If you take the time to ensure a good match in the beginning, the rest becomes easier.

Many of us have made matchmaking mistakes in the past. The impressions that we formed in the interview turned out to be quite a different reality once the person arrived. Even with existing employees, our assumptions about what direction people want to pursue aren't always on target. Even though we know that beginning with the right mix of people is critical, many managers aren't sure how to make that happen. During the interview we tend to talk too much, ask leading questions, or fail to listen. We also fail to help the potential employee learn as much as possible about the team, job, and organization. Both may end up with little real data to base their decisions on and rely more on instincts. The costs of those hiring blunders are high.

Of course, you shouldn't disregard your intuition, but there also are some steps you can take to better ensure a good fit. As with your

A Critical Matchmaking Job

Who do you trust to help raise your children? How do you find the right person to care for them when you can't be there? Some families turn to a professional to help them find the right nanny. These agents try to make a good match, pairing nannies and families who share similar views of the nanny's role, style of discipline for the kids, needed skills, and other aspects of the work relationship and environment.

So, what does a matchmaking professional do? First they meet with potential families and job candidates. Each answers detailed questions about preferred hours, activities to do with the kids, salary, travel requirements (or not), and other special requirements. After completing screenings of both parties, the professional suggests an initial pairing.

During the matching process there are a series of interviews that allow for additional personal contact. The initial interview is held at a neutral location outside the home and allows the nanny and the parents time to chat, seeing how they like one another. This is followed by time spent in the home with Mom, Dad, and the children, which helps the candidate see the dynamics of the home. Additionally, the first interaction between nanny and children happens with the parents nearby. If both sides are still interested, the nanny then spends some time alone with the kids, a type of trial period where experts report it's typical for them to click or for everything to fall apart as preferences and personalities emerge.

Even with this extended interview process, not every detail gets covered. When a nanny joins a family there is a mutual adjustment period where they work out the real work. It's a highly personal relationship they're forming, and in spite of the careful groundwork they've laid, sometimes the job isn't as advertised. Take for example the family who promised to provide a car for the nanny's use. Fine, except the car was the father's, and to use it, the nanny had to arrive 30 minutes early to take him to a commuter train station, and the family didn't want to pay her for the 30 minutes spent daily carpooling Dad. Or consider "the screamers" who believed in loud, vocal confrontation to every problem. This didn't sit well with the new nanny—a calm, reserved woman who gave hugs, not swats. In these cases, the parties hadn't clearly represented what they needed in a match. In the first example, they came to an agreement about the car. In the second, the nanny resigned six weeks in and the agency found her a better match.

Matchmaking professionals don't like starting the process over any more than the families and nannies do. They suggest strongly that both sides create a specific written agreement laying out what each side expects and will do. Because not every point will come up at the start, forming a good working relationship with clear communication channels is essential. As with any employment relationship, fit and trust form a strong foundation for success.

own team, you should try to understand someone's personality, preferences, talents, skills, and aspirations. Ask questions about what the person has enjoyed doing in the past. Offer information about the role: likely time demands, types of tasks, a flavor of the local culture and work environment. Try to answer honestly the questions that are asked. The idea is to start building trust and help the person make a good decision. Unhappy people aren't usually inspired. A "realistic job preview" can stave off some unhappiness. You may not be able to completely understand everything about an individual's aspirations and needs within the selection process; however, you can take responsibility for helping an applicant learn about you, the team, and the work they'll be doing together.

1. Identify what's important to you and to the team. Why are you adding someone to the team? You may have a larger scope of work or more volume. Consider what skills, knowledge, or prior experience you hope to gain with the new addition. There are likely some primary and secondary roles you would like for her to play, so identify the "have to have" versus the "would be nice to have." Chemistry is also important. What is the team's "personality"? Think about how you can balance the benefits of diversity with preventing a poor fit.

Also, don't assume that all team members have the same view of what the team needs in a new addition. Talk it through. People have different areas of focus and priorities even within the same team, and may have varying opinions about what levels of skill and experience are needed. Try to enter the process with some alignment about what you are seeking.

2. Begin with aligned goals, preferences, expectations, and aspirations. Explore the following with the applicant (and the ultimate new hire):

- *The current work of the team and what role this person wants to play or could play in the future.* Create a realistic picture that describes both the most exciting and the least exciting aspects of the team's work. Don't wait until people come on board to mention any potential downsides. (They may think it's a plus!)
- *The environment and culture within the team and the larger organization, and what this person is looking for.* Ask questions that encourage him to describe work environments in which he's felt most comfortable in the past. How does that compare to your company's environment—the opportunities now and in the future, likely timetable for promotion or change, and the person's aspirations? If the applicant wants your job within three months, and a role like yours won't open for two years, then you may have a motivation challenge-in-the-making if you hire this person. Or, if you are hiring someone specifically to grow into a larger role, then it won't work out well to hire someone interested in a stable, predictable job and then hope to persuade him later.

3. Don't leave their orientation to chance. How well can you represent the company? Someone new will look to her manager to articulate what the organization is trying to do today and where it's going in the future. She'll look to her team to help make sense of the organization's culture and politics. You first need to screen for fit, then you and your team will need to help your new team member feel comfortable and be able to contribute quickly.

This doesn't happen magically. Those first few days, weeks, and months are critical to helping people with this process. Concerned with the high turnover ratio they were experiencing several years ago, FedEx took a closer look between what was happening after people said yes to employment. Many of the problems could be traced to new hires' orientation during their first few days on the job (Cook 2002).

Two of the top reasons for turnover in the first six months of a new job are that the job or environment was not what the employee expected, or there was a mismatch between what the job required and what the employee was capable of doing (Branham 2005). These mistakes could be avoided by taking care to clearly explore these elements early on.

YESTERDAY, TODAY, TOMORROW

Psychoanalyst Erik Erikson's theory of the eight developmental stages of man covered a human's entire life span, from infancy to older adult. It focused on how social interactions help develop our personality and sense of self, and ultimately affect our behavior. Recognizing that the major chapters of young adult, middle-aged adult, and older adult are actually comprised of smaller phases and life-defining events—subchapters, so to speak—helps you better understand some of the forces that can shape your people's choices, approach to work, and ultimately, their motivation.

The nature of today's workforce makes awareness of life chapters and phases both more important and more complex, because it's not unusual to find yourself managing three or four different generations of workers. We define them in terms of birth decades and labels like the baby boomers, born in the 1940s and 1950s, the Me Generation of the 1960s, the Gen Xers of the late 1970s and 1980s, and the Gen Yers born toward the end of the last millennium. Their life experiences, culture, values, and views of work are different. They include those who've grown up on the Internet and are beginning their first "real" job, those who are eagerly climbing to the next level of responsibility, those who are more experienced and striving to protect their time outside of work, and even formerly retired people who are returning to the workforce with different goals and limits than they had the first time around.

What does all of this mean for the workplace?

- A person's career will have a different priority level compared to the other aspects of his or her life—such as family, health, leisure, or finances—at different points in time.
- Two people may be employed in the same role, but view the position differently. Consider how this job fits in their plans. Are they short-timers or settling into a long career? Is this the first step on the way to a larger goal, or is this the perfect job and exactly where they want to be long term?

Finally, pay attention to the smaller subchapters that are happening in people's lives. Are they transitioning from the flexible schedule of a college student to the more delineated world of meetings, schedules, and deadlines? Are they the sole provider while a partner completes his or her education? Are they adjusting to becoming a parent for the first time or going through a painful divorce? Are they pursuing a personal goal like running a marathon? Have their adult children moved out, opening up new time and space? Within the bigger scheme of things, what's going on in your employees' worlds may have a ripple effect across the various pieces of their life, including work. They may have a different focus, different interests, and different needs depending on that stage. Understanding what is happening in someone's life may help you adjust the work environment to match what he or she finds motivating at this stage. See our book *Staying Focused on Goals and Priorities* to learn more about life domains and subchapters and how they affect our choices and priorities (Duke Corporate Education, 2006).

Aspirations: Where They Want to Go

Finally, turn from where they've been and where they are today to what their goals and aspirations are for the future. How would they like to see their role and skills develop? Consider how you can help them achieve those aspirations.

"He's never been the same since he came out of his shell."

www.CartoonStock.com

In 1991, when the Library of Congress surveyed more than 2,000 readers asking which 25 books had most shaped their lives, the only business book on the list was Richard Bolles's *What Color Is Your Parachute?* The title that Bolles says he jotted down as a reminder to discuss the topic of why people were "bailing out" of his organization has become one of the best-selling books ever for job changers and seekers. One of the core messages of this guide is to first figure out what you really like to do and what you do well, and then start your search for the job or organization that best matches you (Pink 1999).

This message is just as valuable for those who aren't seeking to make wholesale career moves, but who are simply working to better understand and align their talents, competencies, and future goals with the objectives and opportunities in their organizations.

Beginning with the right mind-set and focus is the first important step. When a Gallup poll posed the question *"At work do you have the opportunity to do what you do best every day?"* to 198,000 employees across 36 organizations, only 20 percent felt that their strengths were being used every day. They also found that 80 percent felt somewhat miscast in their role. To compound the problem, most of their attention and training were being focused on their weaknesses rather than their strengths (Buckingham, 2001).

Don't assume that understanding what people do best and enjoy most is as simple as asking the question. As evidenced by the more than 6 million copies in print of *What Color Is Your Parachute?*, a lot of people need help finding answers. Sometimes this means observing and pointing out the talents and capabilities they may take for granted, such as conflict management, organization, problem solving, or good writing skills. When something comes easily to us, we may not recognize its value or potential application in the workplace. Help people to acknowledge their strengths, and begin to think about how they could use or extend them to achieve their goals.

Build on strengths rather than trying to fix weaknesses. If your employees would like to move into a role that can take advantage of or further develop their strengths, what will it take to get there based on where they are today? Help them create a plan for what they want to do using the following:

- *Education.* Are there certification requirements they must meet? Are there basic courses that will help them learn more about whether this is the right path for them?
- *Exposure.* Consider pairing someone who is interested in a new area with a more senior person in that area who he can observe and learn from. Assuming the role of apprentice can enable him to get a taste of the job without assuming full responsibility.
- *Experience.* As any athlete or performer will tell you, learning on the sidelines is helpful, but eventually you need real-world experience to practice your skills. When you think they are ready, give them a safe opportunity in which to experiment.

A good rule of thumb: Too little challenge leads to boredom, too much challenge leads to frustration, and the right balance generates energy.

BUILD THE RELATIONSHIP

You understand the need to learn more about the identities, chapters of life, and aspirations of your people in order to align them with the opportunities that will be most inspiring and rewarding for them. But how will you accomplish this? You won't know everything about them all at once, but you will learn more and more as the relationship develops and to the extent that they are willing to share (and to some degree, the extent that you are willing to share with them, too).

Like all relationships, it takes time and effort to get to know someone well and to maintain the connection. Relationships don't happen overnight, and they certainly don't develop through a once-a-year performance review. They develop through a series of interactions and conversations. The common elements in the steps to knowing more about someone are taking a genuine interest, taking advantage of opportunities to learn more, and being approachable.

You should be sure that your management routine includes regular check-ins, and opportunities to interact and chat with your team members as a group as well as one on one. Most importantly, have a question to ask—maybe just "How are things going?"—and then be prepared to listen. If the phone rings, don't answer it; if an e-mail comes in, let it sit. Take the time to focus on your team.

By knowing your people, you are in turn better able to help *them* see how and where they play a role today, and how their future aligns with the future of the business.

GETTING WORK DONE

"Like it? Well, I don't see why I oughtn't to like it. Does a boy get a chance to whitewash a fence every day?"

That put the thing in a new light. Ben stopped nibbling his apple. Tom swept his brush daintily back and forth—stepped back to note the effect—added a touch here and there—criticized the effect again—Ben watching every move and getting more and more interested, more and more absorbed. Presently he said:

"Say, Tom, let me whitewash a little."

Mark Twain, The Adventures of Tom Sawyer

During the course of that single afternoon, Tom Sawyer was able to bankrupt nearly every boy in the village willing to pay for an opportunity to have a turn at whitewashing the fence. Would the same tactic have worked again the next day or with a different chore once they realized it wasn't really what they preferred to be doing? Not likely. There is a time-proven saying: People don't quit companies; they quit managers. And sometimes it's because they don't feel the manager knows them, cares about them, or will help them to meet their own goals and aspirations.

On the other hand, there are managers who have people so loyal they'd follow the manager from Peru to Timbuktu, if needed, just to continue working with that manager. Why? *Because those managers can find opportunities that resonate with their people.* These managers can excite them, and connect them to experiences that are challenging, or fun, or help them grow. These managers can match the person's interests with what the organization needs done. Tom Sawyer was able to temporarily convince the other children that whitewashing fences was fun in order to match *them* to his needs, but it's unlikely that the tactic worked once their own interests took over.

It is inspiring when someone can do what he finds most rewarding *and* know it's valued and recognized in his organization. It's demoralizing to work hard at something that doesn't matter. As a manager, you have to help your people feel a sense of achievement and dignity. Both happen when you hear their aspirations, understand how they map to your organization's strategy and roles, and can shape roles that fit your people well.

Periodically, you should take stock. Meet with your boss to get a strategic update. Continue to meet with your team to understand where they are in their lives and careers. Then, ask yourself:

- What are the knowledge and skills my team needs to do its work today?
- Given what I know, how will that list change in the next year?
- What talents, skills, and preferences do my people have now?
- What are the gaps between what we need to accomplish and what we are currently capable and most inspired to do?
- How do I close those gaps—adjust work assignments within the team, help someone grow, hire in new members, or borrow people from elsewhere in the organization?

To get the results you promise, you may have to assign people to some work they don't particularly enjoy or find inspiring. Ideally, people would only do what they love; in reality, people have to do a mix. Good managers aim to keep the proportion skewed in favor of what people love to do, but everyone will have to do some less desired tasks.

As the team leader, you have some latitude in assigning tasks and accountability in a way that recognizes and leverages your team members' diverse capabilities, preferences, and aspirations. No small task in itself. When a task is universally unpopular within your group, rotate among people or set a time limit based on future opportunities. A leader we work with says, "People can stand anything . . . as long as they know when it will end." Let them know what's coming and what role they can play at that time.

You might also encourage some exploration to uncover hidden talents or interests. Someone might have a potentially high intrinsic interest in some activity and never realize it, unless encouraged to experiment. For example, many students have had the experience of coming to love a required course that they thought they would hate. We *start* some activities because of the external incentives (being paid well for it or wanting to work with a particular mentor) but *continue* because we like the activity. Thus, you may need to initially entice people to some new activity, but the importance of the external payoffs diminishes as the intrinsic satisfaction grows: "I do it because I like it" or "because it's morally right."

Keep in mind that doesn't necessarily mean charting a course for people that takes them in a new direction that *you* think they should aspire to. This is about matching people to what *they* prefer to do. Sometimes people find a comfortable niche that is exactly what they want to be doing and where they contribute well. It may be just for that chapter of life, or it may last longer. When the New York Stock Exchange opened for the first day of trading in 2006, Michael Pascuma, Sr., got to ring the opening bell. He was the oldest trader at 96 years old, and had been commuting to his job on the trading floor from his home in Queens for 80 years. In talking about how much he has enjoyed his time there, Pascuma commented, "It must be terrible to wake up in the morning like some people and say, 'Geez, I gotta go to work again.'" He is someone who genuinely loves his work and doesn't want to change his role. (Martinez 2006).

For those people who truly enjoy their work and want to continue doing it, you can still find opportunities that allow them to further develop their skills or add some additional responsibilities without giving up the things that they love to do. If they like, you can offer them challenge and variety or ask them to mentor and coach others who are still learning. You can help match them to work in other areas as tasks or projects shift.

How do you best make these and other opportunities happen for your people? You can purposely position yourself to know what's happening in the organization and the environment. You can be aware of the projects, customers, research, or strategic plans that exist today, and can learn to anticipate what opportunities are coming. If you do this, you and your team will have the chance to take advantage of them.

Those who are "in the know" usually have strong informal networks, with broad spans across their organization or industry. As a leader, you should build a network that facilitates knowing what's happening and where. Interact with a range of people—different functions, different companies, and different geographies. When you share information, ask questions, and build relationships, you position yourself and your team for future opportunities and success.

CHAPTER FOUR

CREATING THE ENVIRONMENT

IN THIS CHAPTER

How Not to Do It ■ Life in Your Neighborhood ■
Get Creative with Systems ■ Become a Catalyst for Change

Understand the Person + **Adapt the Environment**
= Inspired Behavior

In truth, the intrinsic motivation that we all possess doesn't just "go away," but it can be either nurtured and strengthened or neglected and weakened by the leadership and environment that you create for your people. Inspiring leaders do more than connect people to tasks; they supply context, resources, and support for their work, as well as an environment that lets them get on with it. In too many cases, the environment that has been created is working in direct opposition to this approach.

HOW NOT TO DO IT

Bankruptcy is an increasing trend among some U.S. industries, including airlines, automotive suppliers, and automotive firms. Organizations that were once the paragons of industrial strength are engaged in the humbling exercise of protecting themselves from creditors while they attempt to get their businesses straight. Explanations for the problems in the automotive industry range from retiree pensions and medical costs, to significantly lower labor costs in other parts of the world, to weak implementation of lean manufacturing processes, to poor product design, to the liabilities of an installed dealer base. Explanations for the problems with the airline industry include exploding fuel costs, medical and retirement costs, inflated salaries, inappropriate route models, and cost of security. All of these suggested explanations have merit, but we think that the heart of the problems confronting these industries may stem from some deep contextual challenges that prevent their people from feeling motivated. In the next few pages, consider a few of the problems in these two industries.

Weak Manager–Employee Relationships

As we stated in our guiding principles, inspiring others depends on how well you know them and are able to match work to their talents, aspirations, and needs. The dilemma is that the fundamental relationship between boss and employee in these industries belies any such effort. Unions in the United States had their origins in an effort to limit the abuses of management; labor was defined as separate from management with an inherent presumption of hostile intent on the part of managers. Workers formed unions and elected leaders who built a wedge between employees and their firms, a wedge between management and labor. This tension was historically justified as managers *did* engage in abusive practices, often because the presumed core asset of a firm was capital—in the form of an expensive plant, or technologically sophisticated equipment. People were considered a less valuable component of the success of the business.

What started for legitimate reasons has become the de facto world view: Managers should not be allowed to develop a relationship with employees because they will only abuse it. This trend was exacerbated by the very legitimate efforts to create fair work practices for everyone. Intimacy became equivalent to cronyism.

The challenges that unions and fair human resources practices face have not gone away. In some firms, employees are still seen as extensions of machines, less critical than capital, and disposable at will. A simple example is the ease with which firms ship labor-intensive jobs overseas. Managers still do have biases and prejudices that get in the way of fair practices. The continuing compensation differences between men and women are a prime example. The problem is that the cost of the solution is prohibitive. Our language of management, much of human resources practice, and the predominant culture in large firms often diminish our ability to create the relationships through which we can come to understand our employees' aspirations and dreams. Even if we did, the bureaucratic processes by which promotions, work processes, and developmental opportunities are determined limit a manager's ability to advocate for her employees or create a link between real interests and work.

Performance-based Compensation

For most managers, if there is anything clear about the principles of motivation, it is that pay should be performance based. Those who perform best should get paid the most. To some, this is the fundamental premise of good management. After all, research since the advent of behavioral psychology has illustrated that behavior follows incentive, be it cheese for a rat or pay for an employee. Not only is it good psychology, but it is, for many, the central tenet of a capitalist system. However, it is also wrong, both in principle and in application.

Consider the application first. Work has a natural market value, increasingly set at a global level for some industries. What a firm can afford to pay someone is really determined by what other firms pay someone with equivalent skills in the relevant labor market. For automotive firms, the labor market tends to be global. Airlines have it somewhat easier; because they have a fixed locale, their labor markets are more regional. However, the labor prices within the automotive industry and within established airlines are out of alignment.

Over time, the practice of recognizing employee performance through increases in base pay has caused jobs to become compensated beyond their actual market value. People would be willing to do the work for much less, as evidenced by start-up airlines, but the straight-forward practice of baking past performance into base pay has meant that long-tenured employees are paid more than the company can sustain. This was okay as long as all firms played by the faulty principles, but with the advent of global trade in the automotive industry and de-regulation in the airline industry, the flaw has become obvious. The problem is with both the principle and the practice.

The Consequences

One result of the previous two points is that within many large organizations employees are not focused on their work per se, but on their bosses' preferences and whims. Compensation is determined by the boss, not by the market value of what people do, so employees focus the most energy on trying to please their bosses.

Another consequence is that people don't have an external standard of success to inspire them. Rather, an employee's performance is measured according to his boss's expectations, or the performance levels of coworkers, or whether they have improved on last year's numbers. Using internal standards makes the process personal, and often arbitrary.

What's the solution? These industries have seen every fad available to improve employee performance, each focused on a part of the issue, but flawed by their incompleteness. Empowerment, quality checks, Six Sigma, heavyweight teams, process engineering, and other stylized solutions have led to incomplete answers and cynicism as many of the initiatives fall short or quietly fade away. The answer resides in the key principles provided within this book.

LIFE IN YOUR NEIGHBORHOOD

We've all seen the image of the kitten, claws gripping a tree limb, with the phrase "Hang in there, baby!" prominently printed below, or the photo of penguins, with the tagline "Together we can." Of course, there are also the more "serious" motivational images—a rowing crew pushing to the finish line or a climber celebrating at the top

Mount Everest. Boldly printed impact words like Success!, Teamwork!, or Commitment! are added to ensure the message is delivered. They're seen in countless offices, company break rooms, and over the water coolers—any place open for "inspirational filler." These "motivating" posters and plaques are big business. One major supplier reported annual sales of $50 million in 2004, counting on sales of its pithy sayings and warm, fuzzy images to companies seeking to boost employee confidence, productivity, and work ethic.

In reality, these images do little to create an inspiring environment or to boost performance. In fact, they may end up having the opposite effect. As noted in a *Wall Street Journal* article, "When management hangs one up, though, watch out. It's not just that the posters, with their bucolic settings and sports photography, are likely to be out of place in synthetic and non-athletic workplaces. More galling is the notion that motivation can be outsourced and prepackaged, requiring no more managerial effort than buying flip-flops from Lands' End" (Sandburg 2004).

Inspiring others takes work. Every day, you create the local culture and environment for your team and your people. You shape the norms, set the agenda, and lead by example. You affect whether it's safe to experiment with new skills and processes, whether people should wear casual or tailored clothes, or if your team and you have formal or informal interactions. In short, you set a tone for the work environment.

> *The power of the charismatic leader can be effective in the short term . . . However it's not necessarily a sustainable approach. Let's face it, the majority of us don't fall into the same category as Gandhi or Churchill. Motivation is primarily intrinsic, developing within oneself, so depending on others to ignite your motivation is usually short-lived.* (Grazier 1998)

What makes an effective leader? Theories and research on this topic are never in short supply. The "great person" theory asserts that some people just "have it"—that special combination of attributes that enables them to inspire and lead the masses—although comparisons of great leaders' personalities and characteristics haven't been able to demonstrate a proven recipe for success. On the other hand, the "great opportunity" theory is based on the belief

An Inspirational Leader

Captain Mike Abrashoff, former commander of the USS *Benfold,* is credited with transforming this ship from having one of the worst to one of the best performance records in the Navy. Recognizing that most of his crew were young people, many of whom knew what they didn't want, but not quite what they *did* want, Abrashoff's philosophy was to get to know the crew in a meaningful way—who they were and where they were coming from—and then matching that knowledge to the ship's purpose.

Within two days of their arrival, Abrashoff would sit down with new crew members and try to learn something about each of them. He asked questions about why they joined the Navy, what their current situation was like, and what their future goals were. He also asked about their work on the *Benfold*—what they liked least to do and what they would change if they could.

From those conversations, he learned more about what most motivated them among the ship's tasks and which they found most onerous. One of the least valuable chores that, coincidentally, sailors hated most was chipping and painting. Because metal ships sit in salt water, they rust; every couple of months the sailors were spending entire days sanding down rust and repainting the ship. Abrashoff's response was to explore what he could do to alter the environment. He replaced the rusting nuts and bolts with stainless steel hardware and implemented a rust-deterrent and painting process that would last for 30 years. Relieved of this chore, the sailors had more time to learn their jobs and explore other tasks that were more motivating (LaBarre 1999).

that great leadership is a product of skills that can be learned. There is supporting evidence that leadership has more to do with a leader's ability to create the best environment for people than with the leader's personality (Thompson 2004).

Great leaders understand that although the intrinsic motivation that drives behavior comes from within, they can influence the external environment, which can provide inspiration. Inspirational lead-

"Put me on the intercom. It's time for the Morning Motivational Roar."

www.CartoonStock.com

ers use what is within their purview and capabilities to affect a mood, connect to a core passion or value someone has, link to a deeply-held need, or create a task that is so interesting, fun, or challenging that an individual or group feels compelled to act. These leaders work to create an environment that can incite action and provide the stimulus for that internal motivation to grow and continue. Leaders create the local environment for their people; that environment can help the people feel inspired to pursue the things that most motivate them.

As we've talked about, a key element to motivation is in knowing what's important to a person. How can managers create a supportive and inspiring environment without first connecting and closely interacting with their team? It would be difficult.

What type of environment can a manager create that is most likely to build on and further inspire the motivation that people already possess?

- *One that connects individuals to the strategy and creates meaning in ways that work best for them.* Although people certainly have different sources of motivation, few are ever inspired by a direction they had no part in formulating or don't understand. Encourage the ideas and thoughts of your staff to help define goals and action plans, explore problems, and generate innovative solutions. People should be encouraged to explore their ideas, and perhaps see them incorporated or understand why they weren't.

- *One that encourages diverse approaches and contributions, and invests in people's unique talents.* People will play different roles and take different paths in achieving results. An inspiring environment allows individuals to contribute in ways most motivating to them. Arm them with an action plan that they've helped to create and the flexibility to take their own approach in arriving at the target. Try to create a collaborative environment, give them what they need, and then get out of their way.

- *One that uses all the tools and resources available to your advantage.* You won't be able to fully meet every individual work preference or recognize all extraordinary effort with a large raise. Understand that and use the levels that you *do* have in creative ways. For example, when someone makes a key contribution to a successful project, recognize her effort in a way that further inspires the energy and motivation that she already has. That might include arranging an opportunity for people to see the results of their work in action or shifting funds so that they can attend a conference where they can interact with other leaders in their field.

- *One that looks beyond the boundaries of your team to enable people to pursue the work that is most motivating to them.* Be aware of other opportunities in the organization and find ways to match people to work that they are well suited for, even if it extends beyond your team.

- *One that shares the organization's stories.* Although we can be inspired in many different ways—a book, a painting, an innovation—true inspiration often comes when you get to know a person and his story. It may be how he overcame a lack of resources, discovered an unknown talent, or got past a major mistake. Hearing others' stories can help to fuel our own motivation.

It Can Be Difficult, But Not Impossible

Under ideal circumstances, a manager would have time and regular contact with her people, would be able to interact formally and informally, and would have time to check in often. However, we don't live in an ideal world. Managers today often face additional complexities in working with their teams. Not everyone is in the same place, the pace of work and change is rapid, and teams can span formal units. In short, to create the "local" environment, managers must contend with distance, speed, and boundaries.

Managing some team members from a distance can make it more difficult, but not impossible, to know those individuals as well as you would like, or to be fully aware of whether they are matched with the opportunities that are the best fit for them. You may wish to create more opportunities to interact with them one on one than you do with other team members.

As the speed of work increases, be careful to keep the communication lines open, but efficient. A fast pace often means more—more e-mail, more phone calls, more meetings, more projects, and more people to interact with. In our effort to keep up and fit it all in we push faster technology at the problem. Keeping the communication lines open doesn't necessarily mean that you have to make time for every *possible* communication. Take care to maintain positive relationships and be accessible to your people, but at the same time be selective about how you spend your time. When you do communicate with people, recognize that you need to both speak and listen.

Inspiring beyond boundaries and without formal authority may be one of the easier tasks you can achieve as a manager. Have no doubt that your choices, actions, and behavior will influence and impact others. Ideally, your shadow of leadership also will be inspiring. Arlene Blum chronicled in her autobiography her passion for mountain climbing and for fighting the barriers faced by women of her generation. Her accomplishments include leading the first female teams to climb Denali and Annapurna, and setting the altitude record for American women on Mount Everest. Although part of her own inspiration grew from a relative's prediction that she would "amount to no good," Blum was surprised how far her own influence reached. For example, she didn't understand why she received invitations to watch U.S. space shuttle launches, until she learned that astronaut Ellen Ochoa had found inspiration to pursue her own career after attending one of Blum's lectures (McHugh 2005).

GET CREATIVE WITH SYSTEMS

Even though you create the local culture for your team, you don't operate within a vacuum; you also have to work within the larger organizational environment. The industry is fixed, the upper-level managers determine the strategy, and your team's role is for the most part already described. The organization also has processes and systems that you and your people must use. Hopefully, though, you can use them to your advantage. Part of inspiring your team is what you say, and part of it is the *context* you shape for them.

There is a discipline called industrial engineering, and part of that field looks at how the physical environment can affect how people behave. These engineers study how they affect the flow patterns through amusement parks, particularly the lines people wait in for rides—for example, which patterns make people feel like they've moved the quickest through the line. Most of us, though, don't have industrial engineers to design our environment and systems. We have what the organization provides and requires. However, you can bring to bear what does exist, or help create new routines and systems.

Many of the reward systems in organizations aim to retain workers. Benefits packages are competitive to attract workers, and mostly aim at providing financial security. For the most part, they do that; few people leave a job due to bad life insurance, for instance. However, these systems generally are not designed to *inspire* people. Even the much-touted stock options don't directly correlate to higher motivation in most employees. Few individual contributors in large multinational organizations would say that their work directly and significantly affects their company's share price.

Managers have the discretion to find creative ways to inspire people. Don't expect the goal-setting process or performance review or reward system alone to lead to stellar results. Find ways to go beyond that. If we start with the people, then it follows that part of the manager's job is to adapt the organizational environment to match people's motivational needs. An organization should be a context to perform in. Managers set a context (create the environment) and make strategy meaningful, then allow people to fit themselves into it. Be prepared to adjust that context as needed.

For example, a manager in a professional services firm had a team who really went above and beyond on a project. They had worked long hours, holidays, and weekends for several months, some having spent weeks away from home. At the end of the project, the client was thrilled with the result, and the manager wanted to reward her team. She spoke with her boss, who said, "We don't do that here." The manager persisted, saying these people really deserved something special; just because they hadn't done it before didn't mean it wasn't worth asking for. The boss reluctantly took the bonus proposal forward, and, to his surprise, got it approved. The manager's team got their bonuses, and the company as a whole instituted a bonus system shortly after that.

BECOME A CATALYST FOR CHANGE

As we argued in our book *Translating Strategy into Action,* managers should find creative ways to make today's systems and processes work for them, but also can and should take ownership of architecting the systems and processes of the future. Systems and policies come into organizations at particular points in time and to solve particular problems. As time passes and conditions change, those systems may no longer match well to what people need to do. Middle-level managers are critical in keeping the systems aligned with the work their people are doing. A key to this is both understanding how systems and processes are working today, and anticipating and prioritizing what the future needs are. First you must understand what is misaligned, and then figure out how to make the necessary adjustments (Duke Corporate Education 2005).

One leader we know used skip-level lunches as an opportunity to interact with employees without their direct boss being involved. Every few weeks, he'd buy a dozen sandwiches, load up a cooler with sodas, and drive to their work site. He and the employees would hang out around the back of his truck and munch sandwiches. This created an informal and friendly environment for the employees to tell the senior-level leader what was on their minds—what they thought was working well and where they were having issues—and to ask him questions. For the cost of a few sandwiches, he was able to build goodwill, get information, and let his people know he cared. Those employees often said they'd go anywhere to work for him again.

As a leader, he was a great listener and a strong advocate for change. He understood how his organization worked and whom to partner with. He was good at reaching out to others and creating alliances. In this way, he was able to fix what was broken. He chose which problems were worth spending his political capital on, and then advocated strongly and compellingly for them. Demonstrating that he cared about the environment in which they operated and would work to fix what needed fixing, inspired others as well.

Integrity and trust are as important as the direction you provide. Your people will trust you and be inspired by your actions when you tell the truth, demonstrate competence, and do what you say you are going to do. Consider how your own behavior affects others, because your people will look to you to define and demonstrate acceptable norms, deadlines, and work habits for the team.

PERFORMANCE REVIEWS: A CHANCE TO INSPIRE

You know the buzzwords—performance evaluation, appraisal, annual review, competency assessment. Did your pulse quicken a bit just reading them? Regardless of the types of systems and procedures we use, the frequency with which we use them, the labels we give them, or the perceived importance of the process, evaluating and communicating how well someone is performing at his or her job is a responsibility that many managers rank as one of their more dreaded tasks. Some claim they would opt for dental work or a tax audit over conducting a performance review.

Yet, organizations consider these meetings and reports essential. Human resources (HR) professionals spend weeks of their time designing systems, teaching people to use them, and ensuring compliance. Surely there is some value in the process? Surely there must be a better way? There can be, although it might be time to rethink the purpose, approach, and desired outcome of these reviews. First, let's look at how many U.S. and European companies approach performance reviews, and explore why they are often uncomfortable conversations. Then, let's consider an alternative way of thinking about this annual or semi-annual ritual and instead make it an opportunity to inspire.

HOW IT'S TYPICALLY DONE

In many organizations, a performance review has three typical steps. First, the employee and manager fill out forms reviewing what the employee has done in the past year. They might compare the person's performance against a list of standard skills he's supposed to have, or a set of goals or targets he promised to accomplish. Then, the two meet so the manager can tell the employee how he did, how he might do better, and perhaps what his salary, bonus, or job grade will be for the next year. Finally, the manager sends the information to HR.

Of course, this is a simplified version of the process that many of you go through. Some organizations use elaborate ranking systems and have each layer of management re-rank the performance assessments from the layer below. Some organizations have quarterly reviews of goals and feedback and only one formal assessment a year. In some cases, managers compare employees to one another; in other cases, they compare employees' work against an idealized standard (relative versus absolute assessment). If performance is poor, then a manager typically creates an improvement plan, specifying what the employee should do differently, presumably to avoid being fired.

WHY MANAGERS FIND IT DIFFICULT

If you are a manager who has experienced being on both sides of performance reviews, you know that it's often no more pleasant for employees; it's frequently noted as one of the least favorite activities for those on the receiving end, too. Why is that? For one thing, it's set up as a time when the manager passes judgment on the employee. So, employees may assume that they are going to hear only the negative comments, wonder if they are being compared to co-workers, and worry that there will be some real surprises. Some fear that personal differences will cloud their work evaluation, or that their salary will be affected or their job put in jeopardy. *It's a conversation that can affect the employee's ego, identity, and financial security.*

Managers often worry about how to deliver positive and constructive feedback. They may struggle with how to *"package"* a number of important messages for those who need a considerable amount of improvement, or be fearful that good performers will

Worst Review Stories

One of the greatest capabilities of the Internet is that it connects people all over the world and allows them to share their experiences and stories on any topic. Being one of the least favorite activities for many, it's no surprise that stories of performance reviews are plentiful. Some sites even sponsor contests seeking the "worst review" tale. The stories pour in. There is the story of the manager who did no performance reviews in order to avoid delivering the news that the company had done poorly and would be giving no raises; the manager who spent 20 minutes reviewing the wrong employee; and the manager who read the evaluation form aloud and completed it as the employee watched. The grand prize winner of one contest was the story of an employee who received his (late) evaluation in the men's room.

Although these worst review stories span the gamut (and are humorous as long as they are about someone else), they also have some characteristics in common. Managers frequently use forms with narrow rating scales, and directly connect those ratings to an annual salary raise. The employee's raise thus becomes the main focus of the conversation. The managers also tend to delay the conversation, let politics and personal feelings interfere, and have little or no training on how to make the process better (Worstreview.com 2005).

read too much into minor suggestions, interpreting them as more critical than intended. Managers may put so much packaging around the messages that poor performers leave the meeting not really understanding the extent of their performance gaps, and good performers may emerge thinking they have no room for improvement.

Managers may also worry about how employees will react to the feedback and what the repercussions might be. Reactions may range from saying little but sulking and brooding later, complaining to coworkers, or responding with outright anger. They worry that their relationship with the employee may be damaged as a result. They worry that disgruntled employees may have a negative effect on the dynamics of the team; and that some employees may respond with even worse performance. Given the possibilities, it's understandable that some managers end up putting too much packaging around performance gap messages.

What are the effects of all this dread and anxiety? First, *both manager and employee tend to delay the process as long as possible,* with other last-minute crises managing to push this meeting off their schedules. Perhaps some of you are realizing that you are behind schedule with this task at this very moment. When manager and employee do get together, the conversation and opportunity is often shortchanged as managers quickly check items off a required list, cite some numerical scores, and announce an annual raise, while their employees nod and decline to ask any questions. Perhaps they share an initial sigh of relief when it's over, but also leave with unanswered questions, nagging concerns, and no real plan for what to do next.

In addition to the actual conversation feeling difficult, the typical situation both people find themselves in is odd. The underlying assumption is that the manager is the judge, that there are some objective criteria to use—an official standard or competency list that accurately captures what the employee does or should be doing. Everyone gets the exact same treatment and criteria; efforts to be fair and equitable often lead to a vanilla approach that denies the unique interests of each individual. It assumes to a point that *people are plastic and interchangeable;* the organization specifies exactly what's required and people should change to conform to those needs. If not, HR can find another person for that slot.

The conversation often feels disjointed, too, because *it has a mishmash of objectives, some contradictory.* It's often feedback, coaching, goal setting, appraisal, and salary setting all rolled into one. So, the manager offers coaching and feedback in the spirit of helping the person improve her skills while in the next breath shifting to score the person's performance. It feels like, "Tell me honestly your goals and flaws so we can work on them, here's some advice and help, and now I'm going to assess and judge you, even though you haven't had a chance to work on those trouble spots yet." Why should an employee be honest about flaws if the manager can then turn around and use that information to deny the employee a raise? There clearly is a misalignment of interests.

The end result is that what *could* and *should* be a productive conversation that is beneficial to both the manager and the employee often becomes a once-a-year scoring event that has little effect on performance. Envision college admissions as being solely determined by applicants answering three set questions. The evaluation is quick, sometimes brutal, and could determine their future career. The judges use the same criteria and standards on everyone, regardless of the specific goals or talents a particular applicant has. And the outcome determines whether the person gets admitted to a particular college, but not where the person *should* be going, that is, where the person would fit best.

Ultimately, it seems that many performance review processes don't do what would be in the best interest of the organization. Rather than being energized and inspired, people can end up demoralized, fearful, or distracted by the outcome, especially if it's obvious their manager hasn't taken the time to learn more about their talents, skills, or interests. True, it's important to understand how well people are performing; however, it may be just as useful to understand what possibilities exist in the organization based on the people working there, and how to better align individuals and work.

"Your sales figures drop off dramatically during the winter months."

www.CartoonStock.com

A DIFFERENT APPROACH

Let's envision a different purpose and perspective on performance reviews, and perhaps a different outcome as a result. Let's start with the people, not the organization. Consider what the person is good at, enjoys, and aspires to, and be aware of what's happening in that person's world. Understand what the organization's strategy is, what opportunities exist in the organization, and what changes may be coming. Finally, *spend the "performance evaluation" time talking about fit.*

What kind of fit should you discuss and consider?

- How the person's current work matches his skills and talents
- How the person's work fits with the organization's strategy
- How the person fits with the team and organization's culture
- How the person's aspirations fit with the opportunities available

If the conversation is about fit, then the action items are about improving fit—either within the team and organization or outside of it. The conversation centers on playing to the person's strengths, rather than how well he can match his behavior to a fixed and standardized list.

Admittedly, you still need to fill out the company's forms. However, it's up to you *how* you frame the conversation and how you run your team. You may not skip the process or eliminate all the anxiety (in fact, a little anxiety is a good thing), but you can structure the conversation and the outcomes in ways that help your employees, you, and the organization.

Start with the Right Mind-set

Even though we may sometimes fall short in our execution, we can start by preparing well for the performance review process. First, recall the guiding principles from Chapter 2 as you begin: Know and build around their aspirations, strengths, and needs; expect excellence in and ownership of their work; and understand their current priorities and focus. Second, all the good advice people have offered still holds: Don't surprise people with new information, offer feedback only on what an employee can and will be able to adjust, and allow enough time for two-way communication. In addition, keep a productive tone and remember what this conversation should be about:

- *Them, rather than you.* If you focus more on what you, the manager, want or need someone else to do and how she didn't meet *your* expectations or needs, the conversation is doomed from the start. This is about understanding fit—your employee's, not yours.
- *Development rather than appraisal.* People have different starting points, develop at different rates, and have different goals. It's important to figure out how the person is progressing on meeting her aspirations. Focus on the ways that the employee can continue to develop and grow as an individual and as a member of your team. Focus as well on how you can help—does this role fit the person's aspirations and talents, does the environment support the person well enough to succeed, and so on.
- *Future rather than past.* You want to spend more time and energy looking forward to new performance goals rather than rehashing previous mishaps or previous successes. If people like where they are and can improve, they need to understand *how*. If they are doing well, they need to think about how they might further extend their skills. Either one helps them prepare for the next opportunity.
- *Process rather than event.* If you keep the first two points in mind, it makes sense that developing someone for the future doesn't happen by talking about that process once a year during a required review. It's an ongoing process that will need your attention on a regular basis.

Do Your Homework

Preparation includes not just having the right frame of mind, but also being ready for the conversation. First, what do you know about the whole person? Have you spent enough time learning more about your team members' preferences and their current situations? If the conversation is about fit, then you should be able to compare the person and the situation. If you don't know enough, use this conversation to better understand where they are, what's most important to them, or what motivates them. Treat the performance review as an opportunity for additional discovery. People change; there may be some key pieces of information that you are missing or aren't paying enough attention to.

Next, do you know what opportunities are opening up in the organization? Be clear what options this person might have that will improve fit. What can you offer during the conversation if the person raises a concern or desire for a better match?

One of the effects of once-a-year reviews is that managers simply can't remember all that's happened by the time they sit down to talk. Be clear what information you're relying on and how accurate it may or may not be: what you have observed firsthand, what the person has told you directly, and what you've heard from peers, other team members, and people outside the organization. Consider how recent the information is and when it was noted—in real time or in hindsight, for example. Consider what it tells you about how well the person fits with her role or team objectives.

Finally, help your team members prepare as well. Thinking about fit may be new for them, too. They may need some guidance in how to approach the conversation. They may not have thought much about where their talents lie, what their aspirations are, or what other opportunities might fit their skills and goals better. They may not be thinking ahead six or ten months to what their lives will hold and if they'll need to change their work environment. Finally, it can be a real stumper for a manager to ask, "How can I help you more?" Set some expectations and offer some structure, so they can come in prepared.

Having the Conversation

Rather than putting one of you in the role of the "deliverer" and the other in the role of the "receiver," begin with a mind-set that this is a conversation in which *you are on the same side*. This isn't about a set of employee goals that have no connection to your own. This also isn't about how well someone is performing to a list of measures that you hold. As members of the same team and same organization, you have connecting goals and are working toward a shared external measure of success. Each of you contributes toward that success. It may be the improved financial health of the organization, increased customer satisfaction, or additional products and services in the marketplace. From the same side, help the individual understand the ways in which he is making a difference and can continue to contribute to that success.

You also are trying to help the person match as well as he can. Perhaps there are other tasks that are more motivating to him, or new areas he wants to experiment with. The assessment you're doing together is about fit; performance will come if the fit is there.

As you're exploring fit and success, offer feedback to help keep the situation in perspective. People often have a skewed view of themselves, either too harsh or too rosy. They may compare themselves to someone more experienced and therefore feel inadequate and ill-suited for their work. On the other hand, some small wins may have given them a false sense of well-being, leaving them thinking they have little to learn. As we discuss in our book *Changing Roles,* even when people are in a place that is the best fit for them, it still takes time to gain experience, build relationships, and gain confidence. Productive feedback, on a regular basis, helps them to understand how they are progressing (Duke Corporate Education 2006).

Lastly, don't forget to *really* listen. We may find ourselves talking too much in what should be a back-and-forth conversation. You and your team member will be trying to understand the current role, whether it still fits well with what the person wants to do and what the organization needs, and what changes are possible if there is some misfit at present. Use active listening skills and periodically paraphrase the conversation, test for understanding, and show you're engaged in the conversation.

DON'T STOP THERE

People often say that motivation doesn't last. Well, neither does bathing–that's why we recommend it daily.
Zig Ziglar

Think about some of the leaders you have worked for, who you most admired and trusted, and the environments that have been most challenging and motivating. Chances are you didn't need to see a yearly evaluation form to tell you how you were doing in your job. Regular interactions and conversations with your boss, team members, or peers were probably already giving you valuable feedback, reducing the likelihood of any real surprises for you or your boss during the performance review process.

That should always be the case. Take opportunities to observe people's progress and make time for opportunities to talk about how they are feeling about their work on a regular basis, and certainly before the next formal performance review.

One of the problems with yearly reviews is that we tend to recall the most recent events, good or bad, and forget some of the key achievements or growth of the past year. You may be focused on the fact that someone has been tardy coming in the past few days and forget how he stayed late on several occasions to satisfy a special customer request. Spending too much time on what's at the forefront of your mind on that particular day can skew the conversation; you might neglect some other topics that would be more helpful in guiding the person's development, such as progress on acquiring key skills, working with their team, or communicating.

Another problem is that when you don't create regular opportunities to check in with people on how they are doing, you can miss the early warning signs that external factors are acting as a negative source of inspiration. Research has shown that a large percentage of employee turnover begins with a single "shock" event. It may be a major mistake with a client, a disagreement with a team member, a trusted mentor being let go, or learning that a peer is making more money. It's not that the event itself is of major proportions, but that it can cause the person to begin questioning his commitment, enthusiasm, and fit within the company. Offer regular opportunities to talk through your employees' questions and offer support and guidance (Holcom 2005).

Finally, people's progress toward goals, objectives, or development opportunities will be gradual and ongoing throughout the year. One person's aspirations may shift, another may need changes to his work schedule, and another may need resources or coaching or to make minor adjustments to her approach. Don't wait a year to see how people are doing or if this is still the best path for them. Help your people throughout the year to continue to fit well. Talking regularly will make performance-related conversations more relaxed and more useful, and they will feel more like help sessions than evaluations.

CHAPTER SIX

SUSTAINING THE ENTHUSIASM

IN THIS CHAPTER

Getting Past the Rough Spots ■ When the News Isn't Good ■
Nothing Stays the Same ■ What Will Success Look Like?

Managers are all-weather coaches. They need to know how to adapt to inspire people every day and in a variety of situations. One of the biggest challenges managers face is sustaining people's enthusiasm—over time and when the going gets tough. We'll start this chapter looking at how to inspire even during the rough spots, and then turn to how to handle well the day-to-day challenge of working with people.

GETTING PAST THE ROUGH SPOTS

Success is not final, failure is not fatal: it is the courage to continue that counts.
Winston Churchill

Even when people are highly motivated, matched with opportunities that align with their needs, and buoyed by a supportive environment, they are still people. No one is perfect and the best-made plans may go awry. When business is booming, projects succeeding, and resources plenty, it's easier to inspire people. During those times there is likely some extra leeway in the system, which means that there are new opportunities and room to experiment (and potentially mess up). When times are tight, though, people have more constraints. And in the course of work, stuff happens, not all of it good. It may be because of poor performance from individuals, inexperience or lack of knowledge, or simply circumstances beyond an individual's control.

When there is a sense of setback or failure—such as a missed deadline, an unhappy customer, a failed prototype, or a lost account—an employee's confidence, energy, and motivation can be undermined. Recall the example of Olympic athletes from Chapter 1. It's during the times that they have to mentally recover and move on—from costly mistakes, injuries, or external distractions—that they rely on their coaches most. It's also at these times that a manager's ability to guide and inspire people will be critical. It's important to deal with the crisis today and for the longer term: first, doing damage control for both the situation and the individual, and then taking steps to avoid repeat occurrences. That includes not only managing the effects of what has happened, but also helping individuals work through the personal aspects of what the situation means for them.

People Make Mistakes

How do you help someone through a major mistake? There are three key steps to take:

1. *Help repair the damage*
2. *Help the person save face*
3. *Ensure it doesn't happen again*

You need to help correct the damage, but be thoughtful about how you proceed. First, manage your own reaction to the situation. During a crisis, people sometimes have a tendency to act first and think later, which won't help and may make things worse. Instead, acknowledge the mistake, but also stop and put the error in perspective. The situation may be frustrating and could have been avoided, but what is the damage *really*? How does this affect you, the other person, or the rest of the team? What are some approaches you can take at this point and what would be the consequence of each? For example, your first instinct might be to step in and correct the problem, but doing so might undermine your employee's standing with a key customer, not give the person a chance to sort it out and learn, and could embarrass and demoralize the person. Doesn't sound like a winning formula, does it? If there is another alternative, it might be worth pursuing.

Your help might be to act as a sounding board for the person, to comment on possible solutions, and make suggestions. You might have to help get other (temporary) resources in place or provide some political cover so the person has room to correct the mistake. You might guide the person in thinking about who else might be indirectly affected and so should be communicated with now to avoid further relationship damage. What's important is that you are supporting the person while still holding him accountable, ultimately helping him learn from the mistake.

Finally, you should put a plan in place to reduce the likelihood of it happening again. You may want to understand better why it happened. Root cause analysis can be as simple as the "five whys"; that is, asking why something happened, and then continuing to ask why to each subsequent response. As a simple example, an employee was late and you worry that this new person may be unreliable. Ask: Why were you late? Answer: My car wouldn't start. Ask: Why? Answer: Because I ran out of gas. Ask: Why? Answer: Because I was here so late last night that I didn't have time to go by a gas station. Ask: Why? Answer: Because a customer was having problems with product ABC, so I stayed on the phone trying to help. By asking why, you discover that the lateness was actually a consequence of dedication.

For any mistake, you will want to understand the root cause to see where to make changes. Understanding the root cause may involve gathering more information. Seek different perspectives without being invasive or betraying confidences. Talk to people who might have useful insights, including current team members, if appropriate, and observe more on your own. Once you better understand the causes, you can act.

Fixing the Process

Sometimes, one person's mistake can reveal a previously undiscovered problem with systems or processes. In these cases, *anyone* could have made the mistake because standard procedures weren't in place

Bad News Doesn't Get Better with Age

Janice was responsible for an important program of work in a multi-national energy company. She was charged with identifying and contracting several specific sets of resources to help solve a problem. One of the areas of expertise would need to come from outside the firm, an area where Janice had few contacts and little knowledge. Janice did have a close relationship with a third-party consultancy, so she sought their help. She'd known them for a long time and trusted them when they promised they could deliver these experts.

As the project went forward, Janice's approach to keeping tabs on their progress was polite and persistent checking. Even though she didn't see results, she didn't push for action or raise a red flag. The end result? Janice found herself, less than six weeks from delivery of the program, hearing that the consultants could not produce the experts they promised.

Frantic, Janice found herself on the phone with her boss late at night describing the situation. His response was:

1. *"Bad news does not get better with age."* Janice's boss immediately wanted to reinforce that his team should deliver bad news early—not late at night in a panic.

2. *"It's not good but it's not catastrophic; no one got hurt, this will not affect share price."* Controlling his reaction and keeping things in perspective also reduced Janice's anxiety. It set a broader context to keep her focused on a larger picture.

3. *"You understand you are accountable for delivering this, Janice?"* Taking the reins away at the moment of crisis will not help Janice develop the skills she needs to manage this type of situation in the future.

4. *"What do you suggest?"* Her boss is willing to support her, but would like Janice to come up with some solutions on her own. Janice, a little calmer now, comes up with two people she can contact for help finding a resource. Her boss adds two more names for her to call, and Janice gets to work on the problem.

Two days later, when the immediate crisis was under control, her boss asks, "Why did this happen?" Janice conveyed that she relied on the consultants to deliver on their promise. Her boss then asked, "Did you tell them (as I did with you) they were accountable to deliver this resource?" Janice thought and noted she didn't, because she'd wanted to preserve the relationship and trusted they would come through.

Janice learned some valuable lessons about relationships, clear accountabilities, and managing mistakes. She'll be better prepared to handle these situations on her own in the future.

to prevent it. We routinely read news accounts of blunders that read like a comedy of errors (at least after the fact), and marvel at how *that* could have happened. Some are simply humorous with little harm done, while others are quite costly and have long-reaching effects.

Once the damage is controlled and repaired, the next step should not be to find *someone* to blame, but to identify what actions could prevent this mistake in the future. Perhaps more information, wider involvement from some key staff, or tighter controls would help. Perhaps crosschecks or confirmations at key points could catch this mistake earlier, and are easily implemented in the future. Even when checkpoints are in place, people can become relaxed with rules and procedures to the point that mistakes still slip through. It may be time to reevaluate how work flows, how and when communication occurs, and who needs to be involved, and then together discuss ways to improve the process. We tend to think of extensive failure analysis as only warranted at a large scale—hospital errors, airline crashes, or failed drug trials—however, exploring even small errors often can reveal critical information (Edmondson 2005).

Helping the Individual

If the problem originates with an individual, consider the options. The person may have panicked and reacted too quickly to a problem; he may have had good intentions but made a poor choice; he may have delegated too much; or he just may have had a blind spot to his own lack of knowledge. All are correctable. If the negative event happened because someone really didn't understand how to do the job, then your goal is to help that person learn quickly. Offer coaching, training, or on-the-job resources to help the person improve.

When the issue is personal, tread carefully. Be as supportive as you can, but recognize your limits and seek help from others who are better equipped to understand and assist with the problem. Refer the person to available employee assistance programs, if appropriate, and consult with your human resources department for additional support.

Occasionally, someone just may not be a good fit for this particular role. If that's your conclusion, and the person agrees, then you need to consider other options. Start by learning what the person would like to be doing, how she sees her own strengths and aspirations. Recall that people tend to be more motivated and successful when they play to their strengths and are working on what they really want to be doing. Understand where the person thinks she'll fit better or make some suggestions in line with her strengths. If it's possible to adjust the work—either the tasks or the environment—then it may be worth trying.

However, there is a time and place to acknowledge that a mistake wasn't a single event but rather evidence of a deeper misfit. Consider whether it may be more appropriate to let the person go or to try to find him a job that is a better fit in another organization. In some ways, helping someone to be in a place that's better for him can be the most inspiring act you can do.

WHEN THE NEWS ISN'T GOOD

Even when individuals or teams are performing well, external factors—such as layoffs, cancelled projects, budget cuts, industry uncertainty, or even the departure of a key mentor or leader—can interrupt their efforts and have a negative effect on their morale and energy. Still, a manager needs to give a clear, consistent message to her people. If you can explain bad news in a way that's honest, as complete as you know it, and that shows how the way forward will look, people are more likely to stick with you.

Consider Maria. She led the sales and marketing group in eastern Europe. Her team had a sales target predicated on their company signing a manufacturing agreement with a local factory. Six weeks before they were to begin their big product launch, headquarters decided to cancel the manufacturing deal. Although the reason was understandable—HQ didn't think the local company's output was meeting the high quality standards they'd agreed to—it meant that Maria's team wouldn't meet their sales targets, and potentially had wasted six months of hard work getting a coordinated launch plan ready to execute. She had to tell her team about HQ's decision and what it would mean.

First Try

Ted had been taking on more and more responsibility for a high-visibility, high-value project in the company. Ted's boss had growing confidence in Ted's abilities, so he decided to delegate and give Ted the opportunity to prepare and present initial thoughts to the senior executive sponsor.

Ted's boss helped him prepare, and Ted seemed comfortable with the task. They went together to a "pre-meeting" to introduce Ted to this executive.

In the presentation meeting, the senior executive asked some difficult and pointed questions that Ted did his best to answer, but he clearly was out of his comfort zone and was not able to give answers with any confidence. At the end of the meeting, the executive asked Ted's boss to stay behind for a minute, and expressed his doubts that Ted understood what they were looking for, and might not be the right person for the project.

Ted's boss assured him, "He gets it; he's just new to this. I will review the planning alongside him to make sure you are comfortable." The executive reluctantly agreed, but Ted's boss was then left with the dilemma of how to convey this message. Ted had worked hard on the project and the presentation, and his boss didn't want him to become discouraged or fearful of trying again.

Ted's boss began by giving him clear and specific feedback—explaining what he did well, and where he needed to improve. Together, they crafted a plan for how Ted would go forward and prepare differently for the next interaction. This approach set a broad context, explained this was a different level of game, and tapped into Ted's motivation to be able to work at the executive level.

When bad news happens, you often are the messenger. Think carefully but quickly about how to relay that news:

- *When and where?* Consider who you tell and where. Calling a formal meeting sets a different tone than grabbing someone in the hallway. Telling people a few at a time leaves open the chance that part of your team may hear the news before you are able to tell them yourself. In Maria's case, she pulled aside her team leaders to brainstorm options ahead of the special staff meeting she called. She hoped they could develop some contingency plans to help the staff continue forward in a positive direction.

- *What does it mean for others?* What are the ramifications of the news you are about to deliver? In some cases, it may mean that work is delayed, or a favorite project is cancelled, or the team will need to work longer hours for a period of time. People tend to hear news and immediately speculate on how it's going to affect *them*. Expect this and provide as much of an answer as you can. Maria reassured her team that she would talk to HR and revisit the team's bonus goals, and that she and the team leads were reopening talks with another manufacturer and were in the process of negotiating with HQ over using a factory in Spain until they could get a local company online. She explained what she knew and what she intended to find out, and proposed how the team was going to proceed.

- *How are people likely to react?* Is the news expected and therefore just confirmation? Will it be a surprise? Some news will generate strong emotions, such as anger, fear, betrayal, or sadness. Provide a safe way to let people express their emotions without doing a downward spiral. Acknowledge the emotions, even your own, and also provide information about the path forward. What happens next is just as important as what's happening now.

- *Keep the communication lines open.* Give people time to react, to think, and then to come back with their questions. Provide updates as you learn more information. In Maria's case, she and her team leads asked the staff if they wanted another meeting and when. She also took more time than usual stopping by people's desks and being visible. And she kept them updated on her conversations with HQ.

When bad situations happen, managers have the chance to win over or alienate their people. By handling a bad situation well, you continue to offer people respect, affiliation, and a chance to achieve. You may not be inspiring people in the way we typically think of the word, but by being honest and approachable, you are more likely to inspire trust and a willingness to stay with it for a time.

NOTHING STAYS THE SAME

Understand the Person + Adapt the Environment = Inspired Behavior

As a manager, you know to expect change and take care not to be surprised and unprepared when shifts occur. You also need to help others sustain their enthusiasm in spite of, or because of, these changes. We just talked about a bad case. Now we turn to managing and inspiring people over time. The formula for creating inspired behavior that was introduced in Chapter 1 is a dynamic one. People and situations change, and so will the fit that best inspires someone. Continue to know the person and continue to adapt the situation to achieve inspired behavior. As we've said earlier, you have to grow and maintain relationships with your team members and periodically take stock. You should provide different opportunities to people, and build and maintain a work environment that supports their efforts (see Chapter 4).

Stay Connected

Over time, we get to know people. There may be a tendency to think we know them better than we actually do, or to assume nothing has changed with them or their lives. However, change is like death and taxes—a sure thing. There may be new people, new projects, new teams, new alignment to the organization, or new aspirations for the people you work with. The possibility for change and therefore the need for realignment are always present. Time and change give you the opportunity and excuse to check in and reconnect with your team.

You may have taken time at a given point to talk with your people. They may have shared, or you've observed, their values and beliefs, their skills and capabilities, their chapter of life, their aspirations for the future, and what work is most motivating to them. How long ago was that? It may be time to reach out to them again.

Periodically create or take advantage of opportunities to interact with people and catch up. Keep them updated on your life and continue to learn about theirs, to the extent they're willing to share it. Events happen that may be leading them to rethink their role at work. For example, a new marriage may lead to thoughts of starting a family. An ailing parent may spark thoughts of moving closer to other family members. Someone else's promotion may spark introspection about a person's own career path and prospects.

This is a challenge for leaders: how to be aware of these events yet not intrude on someone's personal business. Where possible, build a mentoring relationship where the person might come to you for advice or options. Be accessible and nonjudgmental when people approach you. Find time regularly to grab coffee or take a quick walk with individual team members so they have opportunities to raise issues with you. Mention options that may be coming up in the next six months as an invitation. Keep the conversations going. Circle back around and recheck your thinking about where they are and what is most motivating to them. Inspiration is about being a good matchmaker. A good matchmaker has a current picture to work from.

Provide Different Opportunities

As people grow, develop, and change, the intrinsic motivators that drive their behavior can change as well. The types of activities and challenges—creative expression, problem solving, sharing a skill with others—that get someone in a "zone" varies over time. The motivation that someone once felt when engaged in a particular task may no longer be as strong. It may be time to help him recalibrate the fit between his aspirations and what he's doing today. Of course, individuals and situations vary, but there are some common characteristics when the "fit" is right, and people are motivated. If someone feels blah, it may help to provide a different experience. Can you create a better fitting situation with any of the following?

- *Tension.* A little anxiety can be a good thing. The task is important, and there is some level of apprehension and worry whether the person has the ability to complete the task. Rather than tasks that seem insignificant and boring, it matters, and the person's adrenalin is increased. It may be the person is leading a customer meeting for the first time, presenting a new project and budget proposal for approval, or trying to repair a system problem that has temporarily disabled your inventory system. It's a chance to prove herself when the stakes are higher than usual.

- *Challenge.* The person's attention or curiosity is piqued. This is something new that goes beyond his current knowledge or skills. The level of difficulty is enough to stretch his abilities. It may be difficult, but he thinks he can do it. It may be a solitary challenge, such as painting a large mural, or it may be a competitive challenge that involves other people, such as a game of chess or hitting a sales target.

- *Feedback.* When people fit well, they seem to be able to read a situation more accurately. Feedback is more immediate because the person can gauge it herself. Feedback may come from others—the knowing nods of understanding from a peer or the applause of an audience—or it may come from the person's visible progress—having written more sections for a report, improved key metrics, or reached the next stage of a process.

- *Learning.* Attempting and accomplishing a particular task offers an opportunity to grow and learn. The experience enables the person to add to her knowledge and skills. As her confidence and abilities grow, she is then ready to take on more challenging assignments.

The types of assignments and tasks that will provide the right amount of tension, challenge, feedback, and learning for each individual will vary. Knowing more about the whole person will help you in matching each to the right tasks, or in creating specific opportunities for them.

Adapt the Environment

Just as individuals change, so will the teams, divisions, and organizations within which they work. Any number of factors in the external business environment can affect the local culture of your group, including strategic realignments, mergers, regulatory changes, shifts in executive leadership, new technologies, and globalization. These changes are likely and to some extent expected, and their effects will be felt throughout the organization. It's the job of the manager to be aware of when to make adjustments in the local environment. Ask yourself the following:

- Do you actively support experimentation?
- Do your routines need tweaking?
- Do the systems align with the work you team is trying to do?
- Do you offer flexible schedules or locations for work?
- Are you leading the way?

Keep communicating and talking about the work and about what upcoming changes may mean for your team. Encourage your people to experiment and try new tasks and approaches. Provide the resources, coaching, or guidance they need; and give political cover, if needed.

WHAT WILL SUCCESS LOOK LIKE?

What happens when individuals are inspired—how will you know? Even though people are motivated by very different things, we can describe the *general traits* of people who are inspired to do their best work. Take Gabrielle as an example. She gets up in the morning with a smile, eager to get to work at the plant and flower nursery. She knows her customers rely on her to advise them on how to landscape their gardens and create eye-catching floral displays. She knows the junior employees look to her to provide steady work and guidance as they learn about botany, business, and design. Although Gabrielle isn't the only senior staff member, she is the one people seek out most. She is knowledgeable and passionate about what she does.

How do we know Gabrielle is motivated? She takes personal responsibility for the quality of work at the nursery. Although she's not the owner, she acts as if she were, showing care and pride in the business. She understands that her efforts matter to the organization. Customers come to the nursery specifically to work with her, and she helps make this nursery special. Finally, she has energy and effort that take her beyond a narrow job that merely has to be done; Gabrielle envisions what's possible, and initiates improvements and innovations. She often explores with her boss ways to gain a competitive advantage for the nursery.

As a team approach continues to grow across organizations, how to keep teams energized and inspired over the long haul is a huge concern. So many teams are really collections of individual contributors who are called a team merely because they all report to a particular manager. In some cases, this may be appropriate. Their manager can focus on what each individual aspires to and how to meet those goals. In other cases, though, the team really benefits from working as a collective. Those teams and their managers need to consider both the individual needs and the team-level needs. Those managers should inspire the team as a group, and help them tap into what motivates them. So how do we know if a team is working well together and is inspired?

In our experience, motivated teams enjoy what they're doing and whom they're working with. They aim for ambitious results and play to their individual strengths to meet the collective goal. They don't find a challenge burdensome; rather, they see it as yet another chance to "play" and succeed together. They instinctively know that it's easier to accomplish their work when there is camaraderie among team membersrather than discord. They try to understand not just the skills and knowledge of each member, but also to be aware of each other's personalities and preferences. A highly motivated team understands how it directly helps the organization meet its strategic goals.

The cumulative efforts of motivated and inspired individuals and teams can be a key differentiator for an organization. At a time when your competition often has equal access to resources, information, or capital, the value of your people cannot be underestimated. When people are energized by the work that they do, in an environment that inspires them, the organization will see the benefits. Their energy is focused, their results exceptional, and their motivation high.

To be clear, even though the benefits are compelling, the new approaches that we have described here will take courage. You have to realize the job you are signing up for when you become a manager.

It's more than managing systems and processes. It involves real people in real situations.

Focus on getting the basics right and the rest will follow. Take a genuine interest in knowing the whole person, understand the challenges that people are most motivated by, and take the lead in creating an environment that enables them, you, and the organization to succeed. It's likely that you are better at it than you think. And remember, the benefits of getting it right can be huge.

BIBLIOGRAPHY

Ballard, Beverly. 2003. "Performance Review Anxiety." *Harvard Management Communication Letter.* Harvard Business School Publishing Corporation. Article Reprint No. C0310D.

Branham, Leigh. 2005. "Why Employees Leave." *The Globe and Mail.* 27 April 2005.

Buckingham, Marcus, and Curt Coffman. 1999. *First, Break All the Rules.* New York: Simon and Schuster.

Buckingham, Marcus, and Donald O. Clifton. 2001. "The Strengths Revolution." *Gallup Management Journal* (January 2001).

BusinessWeek Online. "Star Search: How to Recruit, Train, and Hold On to Great People. What Works, What Doesn't." 10 October 2005. (Accessed April 2006.) *www.businessweek.com/ @3jN0MocQBRs5EBwA/magazine/content/05_41/b3954001.htm.*

Catlette, Bill, and Richard Hadden. 2000. *Contented Cows Give Better Milk.* Contented Cow Partners, LLC.

Cook, Julie. 2002. "FedEx Expresses Concern for Turnover Rate." *Human Resource Executive®* (April 2002).

Csikszentmihalyi, Mihaly. 1997. *Finding Flow: The Psychology of Engagement with Everyday Life.* New York: Basic Books.

Duke Corporate Education. 2005. *Translating Strategy into Action.* Kaplan Publishing.

———. 2006. *Changing Roles: Avoiding the Transition Traps.* Chicago: Kaplan Publishing.

———. 2006. *Staying Focused on Goals and Priorities.* Chicago: Kaplan Publishing.

Edmondson, Amy, and Mark D. Cannon. 2005. "The Hard Work of Failure Analysis." *Harvard Business School Working Knowledge.* August 22, 2005.

Erikson, Erik. 1964. *Childhood and Society.* New York: W. W. Norton & Company. Reissue edition, 1993.

Farson, Richard, and Ralph Keyes. 2002. "The Failure Tolerant Leader." *Harvard Business Review.* Reprint R0208D. August 2002.

Feldman, Daniel A. 1999. *The Handbook of Emotionally Intelligent Leadership.* Falls Church, VA: Leadership Performance Solutions Press.

Goleman, Daniel. 1998. *Working with Emotional Intelligence.* New York: Bantam Books.

Grazier, Peter. 1998. *Team Motivation.* Teambuildinginc.com. (Accessed January 2006.) *www.teambuildinginc.com/article_teammotivation.htm.*

Herzberg, Frederick, Bernard Mausner, and Barbara Bloch Snyderman. 1993. *The Motivation to Work.* Transaction Publishers. Reprint edition, 1993.

Holcom, Brooks C. et al. 2005. "Shocks as Causes of Turnover: What They Are and How Organizations Can Manage Them." *Human Resource Management.* Wiley Periodicals, Inc. 44: 337–352.

Humphreys, John H., and Walter O. Einstein. 2004. "Leadership and Temperament Congruence: Extending the Expectancy Model of Work Motivation." *Journal of Organizational and Leadership Studies* (Spring 2004).

Jackman, Jay M., and Myra H. Strober. 2003. "Fear of Feedback." *Harvard Business Review.* Harvard Business School Publishing Corporation. April 2003. Article Reprint No. R0304H.

Johnson, Lauren Keller. 2005. "The New Loyalty: Make It Work for Your Company." *Harvard Management Update.* Harvard Business School Publishing Corporation. March 2005. Article Reprint No. U0503A.

---. 2005. "Getting New Managers Up to Speed." *HBS Working Knowledge.* 4 July 2005.

Kelner, Jr., Stephen P. 2000. "Human Motivation and Organizational Mobilization." *Center for Quality of Management Journal* 9 (1). MA: The Center for Quality of Management, Inc.

LaBarre, Polly. 1999. "The Agenda—Grassroots Leadership." *FastCompany*. April 1999. 23: 114.

Lehrer, Jonah. 2006. "The Reinvention of Self." Seedmagazine.com. (Accessed February 2006.) *www.seedmagazine.com/news/2006/02/the_reinvention_of_the_self.php*.

Martinez, Jose. 2006. "At 96, Trader Holds His Own on Stock Exchange Floor." *New York Daily Times*. 12 January 2006.

Maslow, Abraham. 1943. "A Theory of Human Motivation." *Psychological Review*. 50: 370–396.

McClelland, David C. 1988. *Human Motivation*. New York: Cambridge University Press. Reprint edition.

McClelland, David C. and David H. Burnham. 2000. "Power Is the Great Motivator." *Harvard Business Review OnPoint Enhanced Edition*. 1 February 2000.

McHugh, Paul. 2005. "How Blum Managed to Reach the Top: Book Tells Climber's Inspiring Tale." *San Francisco Chronicle*. 15 December 2005, D-8.

Oakley, James. 2004. *Linking Organizational Characteristics to Employee Attitudes and Behavior: A Look at the Downstream Effects on Market Response and Financial Performance*. Forum for People Performance Management & Measurement.

Pink, Daniel. 1999. "What Happened to Your Parachute?" *FastCompany* September 1999. 27:238.

Porter, Lyman, and Edward Lawler. 1968. *Managerial Attitudes and Performance*. Homewood, IL: Irwin-Dorsey.

Rose, Barbara. 2005. "Motivation Misconception." *Durham Herald-Sun*. 27 November 2005.

Rosenthal, Robert, and Lenore Jacobson. 1968. *Pygmalion in the Classroom: Teacher expectation and pupils' intellectual development*. New York: Rinehart & Winston.

Sandberg, Jared. Commentary: "Inspirational Posters Don't Always Produce Anticipated Response." *The Wall Street Journal* (Eastern Edition). 23 June 2004. B.1.

Secretan, Lance. 2004. *Inspire! What Great Leaders Do.* Hoboken, NJ: John Wiley & Sons, Inc.

Senge, Peter M., et al. 1994. *The Fifth Discipline Fieldbook.* New York: Currency.

Thompson, Leigh L. 2004. *Making the Team: A Guide for Managers.* Upper Saddle River, NJ: Pearson Education, Inc. Second Edition.

Wallington, Patricia. 2002. "Error! Error!" *CIO Magazine.* August 1, 2002.

Ware, B. Lynn, PhD, and Bruce Fern. 1997. *The Challenge of Retaining Top Talent: The Workforce Attrition Crisis.* Integral Talent Systems, Inc.

Williams, Kathleen. 1999. "What People Need from a Leader." *Building Passion in the Workplace.* (Accessed January 2006.) *www.kathleenlwilliams.com/whatpeopleneed.htm.*

Worstreview.com. 2005. *Worst Review Contest.* (Accessed February 2006.) *www.worstreview.com.*

Zemke, Ron, Clair Raines, and Bob Filipczak. 2000. *Generations at Work: Managing the Clash of Veterans, Boomers, Xers, and Nexters in Your Workplace.* New York: AMACOM.